W9-COF-947

UP TIGHT!

by JOHN GIMENEZ
with CHAR MEREDITH

WORD BOOKS
WACO, TEXAS

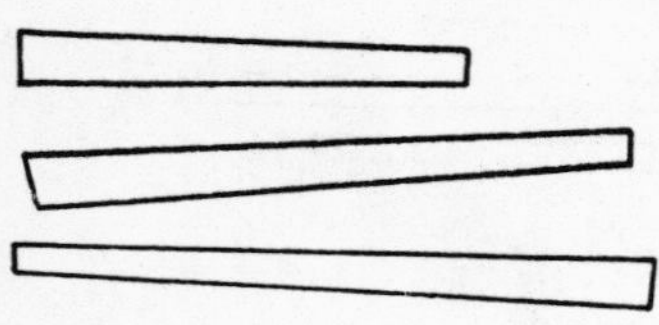

Word Books
Waco, Texas

Library of Congress Catalog Card
Number 67-17825
Printed in U.S.A.

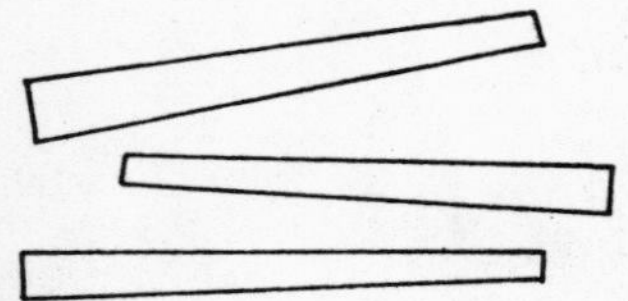

Dedication

We humbly dedicate this book to Rev. Fransico and Leoncia Rosado (Pop and Mom). They gave unsparingly of all they possessed . . . making themselves all things to all men, that they might win some to Jesus.

Pop Rosado has gone on to be with the Father, at the age of 52. He was stricken with a heart attack while trying to revive an addict who had taken an over dose. Two months later, Pop died.

Mom Rosado continues to labor on, fighting the good fight, bearing the cross of her ministry, secure in the knowledge that they who sow in tears shall reap in joy.

They loved us, when they knew us not,
They fed us, when we hungered most,
They kept us, when all doors were locked,
They led us, to the Lord of Host.

Your Children in Christ

THE ADDICTS

a Junkie's Glossary

A JUNKIE'S GLOSSARY

BAG: small packet (like a glassine stamp bag) of narcotics.

BEEF: the charge brought against someone who has broken the law.

BENT: so high on drugs that you stand or sit bent over.

BID: sentence in jail.

BLIND: really, really high.

BODEGA: Spanish grocery store.

BOMBITA: vial of Desoxyn, an amphetamine (stimulant) sometimes taken with heroin for a stronger high.

BOOST: steal.

BOOT: draw the blood up and down in the dropper after injecting the drug into the vein.

BOP: fight.

BOSS: very good, top-notch.

BREAD: money.

BULLS: police.

BURN: shoot (gang); take someone's money (junkie).

BURNT OUT: rendered useless by recognition.

BUSTED: arrested.

CAP: capsule of narcotics.

CAT: guy, man.

CHICKIE: watchman.

CLEAN: no longer addicted.

COLD TURKEY: abrupt withdrawal from drugs without medication.

CON: swindle by gaining a person's confidence.

CONNECTION: street peddler of narcotics; source of supply.

COOKER: bottle top or spoon used for dissolving heroin in water over flame.

COP: buy narcotics.

DEAL: sell narcotics to addicts.

DEALER: drug peddler.

DESOXYN: see Bombita.

DIG IT: understand.

DITTY BOPS: teenager gang fighters.

DOPE: any narcotic.

DUDE: guy, man.

DYNAMITE: heroin of exceptional purity.

FALL OUT: pass out from an overdose of narcotics.

FENCE: a person who will buy stolen goods.

FIX: injection of narcotics.

FLIM-FLAM: switching money so as to cheat, swindle.

GANG - BUSTING: fighting between gangs.

GARBAGE: grossly inferior heroin.

GETTING OFF: injecting narcotics.

GOOF: To nod, to mess up.

GOOFBALL: barbiturate.

GREASY: hooked, addicted.

HABIT: regular use of narcotics.

HIGH: feeling of well-being after taking drugs.

HIT: finding the vein with the needle so as to inject narcotics.

HOOKED ON THE NEEDLE: addicted to narcotics, especially heroin.

HORSE, H, CABALLO, DOO JEE, SCHMECK, TECATA, WHITE STUFF, JUNK: heroin.

HORSE PARTY: group gathered for the purpose of shooting dope and drinking.

HOT SHOT: poisoned heroin.
HUSTLE: the whole pattern of getting money and getting dope; more specific use—prostitution.
ICE: kill.
IN: belonging to a certain group; accepted.
JOHN: a man who buys sex relations with prostitute.
JOINT, REEFER, STICK: marijuana cigarette.
JOHNSON, JONES: the habit.
JUNK: narcotics, usually heroin.
JUNKIE: habitual user of narcotics.
KICK: thrill, excitement.
KICK (THE HABIT): break the habit of using drugs.
KY: Federal Narcotics Hospital in Lexington, Kentucky.
LEMON: an inferior bag of heroin, or a trick bag with nothing in it.
LOAD: an amount of packaged heroin.
MAINLINE: inject directly into a vein.
MAKE IT: be recognized as valuable; to succeed in getting rid of the dope habit.
MAN, THE: police.
MARIJUANA: a drug made from the flowering clusters and top leaves of the hemp plant. It is classified as a depressant, and is the most accessible of all the prohibited drugs.
MONKEY: dope habit.
NARCO: narcotics detective.
NEMBIE: barbiturate.
NOD: be drowsy, to the point of bending over with head between legs.
OD: overdose of narcotics.
OIL BURNER: very big habit.
ON THE HORSE: addicted to heroin.
OVERDOSE: too large or strong a dose of narcotics so that the addict passes out, often dies.
PAD: user's apartment, home.
PANIC: a scarcity of drugs.
PIMP: a man whose business is selling the services of prostitutes.
POT, GRASS, WEED, HAY, TEA: marijuana.
PIECE: one ounce of heroin.
PILLHEAD: addict on pills.
SECONAL: barbiturate.
SHOOTING GALLERY: place where addicts congregate to shoot drugs.
SHORT CHANGE: beat a cashier out of the right change by fast talking.
SICK: physically ill from lack of narcotics, as the effect of the last dose wears off.
SKIN POP: injection of heroin into the muscle, or under the skin.
SPIKE: needle used for the injection.
STICK: marijuana cigarette.
STICK: business; racket; (what a person is best at).
STING: robbery.
STRAIGHT: an addict's feeling of well-being after taking drugs; also used to describe the condition of life after an addict successfully kicks his habit.
STRUNG OUT: to be addicted; badly in need of a fix.
STUFF: any narcotic.
TAKING OFF: injecting narcotics.
TIRED: used up; sick of the habit.
TRACKS: veins collapsed by constant injections. Also needle scars from injections.
TRICK: a man who buys sex relations with a prostitute.
TUINALS: barbiturate.
TURF: the territory claimed by a gang.
TWISTED: out of your mind.
UP TIGHT: trapped; cornered; no way out. Also used to describe a close friendship.
WAKE-UP: morning shot of narcotics.
WASH: beat up.
WASTED: tired; used up.
WORKS: equipment for injecting narcotics.

Prologue

We are "The Addicts." We grew up in the street together; fought in gangs together; shot dope together; broke into local apartments and stores; slept in the same basements and rooftops; got busted together; got put away in the same reformatories and prisons, and finally got delivered because of the same little church in the Bronx.

Each of us has his town story to tell of how he appeased that bitter heroin god. We all found our own ways of "living by our wits." Every junkie has to figure out his own "hustle"—a way of getting money for drugs without working. Frankie began stealing when he was a little kid. Dannie learned to "con" people into doing almost anything for him. Terry and Pee Wee became stick-up artists. Mike ran an extortion gang. Snuffy knew how to "short-change" and scalp tickets. Chuck had girls working for him. I was a pimp and a dealer. I knew all the connections.

But even though we took different paths to obtain dope, we all got dragged to the bottom of the heap by our addiction. We became the outcasts, even in slum society. We were ragged and dirty, careless and wasted. Fear and hatred filled our world.

Contents

section 1 . . . Johnny Pimp

section 2 . . . The Addicts

Part 1:

JOHNNY PIMP

1. Sadly I Await The Dawn

The concrete was cold and wet. It was raining, and it was dark. Wheels splashed by just a few feet from my head. I started to open my eyes but it was too much trouble. I didn't know where I was.

I couldn't remember anything. Someone was bending over me. He was going through my pockets. I wanted to get away from him, but my mind seemed disconnected from my body. When I started to grab his hand I couldn't find it. "What're ya doin'?" I asked.

"Shut up, man!" He kicked me as he got up to go. "Filthy junkie," he muttered.

I wanted to yell at him to leave me alone, but I blacked out again.

When I came to, the combo in the bar was moaning, "I Ain't Got Nobody, and Nobody Cares for Me." I rolled over on my stomach and pounded the sidewalk. The tears rolled down my puffed up face. I was marked—either to die or to be a dope fiend the rest of my life. Hated! The people on the street hated me. My family hated me. I hated myself. And there wasn't anybody anyplace who could help me.

Sure, I seen other guys fall out and die. It happens all the time in the junkie's world. Too much dope for the old body and everything stops working. I don't know why I didn't die. These things are so common in our neighborhood. Nobody gets excited over a dead junkie.

"Just toss him out on the sidewalk. If he dies in here, y'know, we'll be up for murder."

We were drinking wine one night in this guy's pad. We "took off" as soon as his old lady was gone. I just finished taking my shot and it was good, man. Dynamite! I was sitting at the table with a cigarette in my hand. Nodding and watching Tim. He was having trouble finding the vein.

"Help me, man. I can't get a hit."

I laughed. "You don't got no more veins, man. You need a new arm."

He was panting. You can die there, y'know, waiting to get a hit. I helped him tighten the belt around his upper arm. Finally he got the spike in.

"I got it, Baby, I got it." Tim booted it a few times—he got a kick out of watching the blood come up in the dropper, then he'd shoot it back into his arm. Junkies dig that!

He sat down across the table from me. "Good stuff, huh, Johnny? Real boss!"

I took a long drag on my cigarette, and watched him closely through the smoke as he put the wine bottle to his mouth. "Whatcha doin', Baby? You crazy?"

He was nodding. But he came to with a start and wiped the blood off his arm, and stuck the needle in the water glass to clean it. "Man! This place is a pigpen. Gotta get it cleaned up 'fore my ol' lady comes back."

I didn't like the way he looked. "Hey, Baby." I reached over and moved the wine out of his reach. "What the hell's a matter with you? Don't fall out on me!" He looked like he was passing out.

"I'm O.K., Johnny," he was talking so soft. "Just tired. Beat. Wasted. Tired of shootin' dope. Think I'll go to 'KY' tomorrow and get cleaned up. Gonna kick this habit, Johnny. You tell my ol' lady I'm looking for a job. She'll like that. She works awful hard." His head fell forward on the table.

I knew he was in trouble. "Hey, man. Wake up."

"Yeah! I'm tired a bein' a filthy no-good junkie, Johnny. I'm so . . . tired . . . o' all this. . . . " I could hardly hear him. He was breathing funny and I knew he was falling out.

I jumped up and slapped him. "Get up, man. I'm not playing!"

He didn't answer. "Come on, Tim. We go for a walk." But when I tried to lift him up off the chair he fell on the floor. I got a wet cloth and put it on his face. I loosened his collar and took off his sweater. And I cursed all the time I was trying to wake him up. I remember thinking, "This creep has got to go and fall out on me right now. I can't even enjoy my high! I gotta be worried about him!"

But I didn't want him to die. I didn't wanna be there all alone with him. I didn't want "the man" to come and find us. I didn't want to get busted again. I started to cry. I grabbed him up again and shook him.

"I'll kill ya if ya die, Timmy. Get up. Get up, man!"

I didn't know what to do. I threw him down and staggered to the refrigerator for a carton of milk. I held Timmy up and tipped his head back so I could pour some milk in his mouth.

"Drink it. Come on. This'll fix you."

But it didn't. It was too late. Tim's head fell forward and the milk ran out all over the floor. I just sat there holding him. Crying like a baby.

"Tim, don't die. Don't die, Tim. Oh God, please, God. Don't let him die, God."

But Timmy was dead. There were others, too, who had died.

And now as I lay there in the rain, I wished I was dead. I didn't want to get up off the sidewalk. I knew it would be a great help to everybody if I'd just shove off and leave them alone—my mother and father, my wife, my brothers and sisters, my daughters. I brought them nothing but pain and horror and shame. I brought tears to all their eyes. I broke their hearts over and over again. I been nothing but a mess of trouble since I was born.

I been in all the reformatories and shelters—Children's Village, Warwick. Been in all the hospitals in New York and all the prisons. They all know me from 16 years with a big habit. "Here comes Johnny Pimp again." But they couldn't help me. I was no good now. Never had been any good. Never would be any good. That's what they told me.

I was a stinkin' filthy no-good junkie, twisted out of my mind. Up tight. Bound by dope. A chronic addict. A chronic criminal. A chronic liar. There was no way out. The doctors said it. The psychologists said it. The narcos said it. My family said it.

That's the way a junkie's life is, and it sure ain't worth coming back to.

I don't know how long I lay there. It started to rain again and I sat up to see where I was. I didn't care really. But I knew I wasn't dead and I had to start hustling. I was already getting sick—my nose was running. And I knew it wouldn't be long till that "monkey" on my back would be screaming for more junk. It made me mad that I had to come back and get going all over again. I coughed as I got to my feet and started over to the boulevard. It ain't easy to find a dealer to cop from in the middle of the night. I shoulda been glad I could move. But look! man! coming alive to the same old mess is no big kick.

Johnny Gimenez—sighing in the night—couldn't do nothing right, not even die.

Sadly I await the dawn,
Just another day to mourn.
With an empty heart I must stay;
I'm the lamb that went astray.

Through the lonely nights I sigh—
All the world can hear my cry,
And no one seems to know
What to do.

I'm so sad, and oh! so blue;
I walk the streets of sorrow,
My life an endless scene of shame.
I'm lost, I'm lost, I'm lost.

2. A Delinquent Since I Was Born, I Guess

I been a juvenile delinquent since I was born, I guess. There was seven of us kids, plus two half-sisters, in the Gimenez family. I was the middle one and the wildest—the only one that turned out real bad. Called my father a "son-of-a-——," stuck a stick in my sister's eye and made her cockeyed, beat one of the kids with a bat, set fire to the school—used to fight all the time.

My father was half Caribbean Indian and half Spanish, and my mother was half French. They moved from Puerto Rico to Spanish Harlem, and that's where it all began for us. Even though my father was a minister I soon learned to be a little tougher than the next guy, a little wilder. I cursed a little louder, learned how to defend myself. In New York City I soon discovered I had to be "one of the boys" or I wouldn't make it.

I look like my father, but it's always been tough on him to have me named for him. Ramiro is my oldest brother, and when we were kids he was sort of a favorite. Dad wanted to name his first son John—you see, he'd had another son by his first wife, and they called him John, but he died when he was nine years old. When my father married my mother, the first child was a girl, Lisa. Then when the next baby came along, it was a boy and Dad wanted to name him John, but Mother wouldn't accept it.

"No," she said firmly. "His name is Ramiro.

I think her father's name was Ramiro. Anyhow she got her way—I don't think she had her way anymore after that, but they hadn't been married long then. My father never forgot though. He always thought that Ramiro should have been the one named John—because he was the one who was following in his footsteps.

My father had become a minister before they moved to New York, where he took a Methodist church in Spanish Harlem. He was preaching all the time. You could say I was almost born during a sermon. My whole life as a child was in church—almost everyday.

I know my dad used to grab me by the ear and pull me inside and set me down hard on a chair. But before long—during the message—I would slide off the chair and start crawling under the seats, between people's legs, till I got to the back. Then I'd scoot out the door. Father got smart eventually, and had someone sitting in the back—usually my oldest sister, Lisa. Then when I'd get to the last row she'd grab me and haul me up beside her—everytime she grabbed me.

There were always lots of kids in the church—and they were always screaming. The church was in the Puerto Rican district and it wasn't too large. But boy, preachers really got to scream to be heard over them kids. Every family there had at least ten children. Ours was one of the smallest ones, with only nine kids.

Father was very strict. He dominated everyone. And every Sunday he had us all in church—everyone of us had to go. He was a heavy-handed disciplinarian; it had to always be his way. We never had a chance to explain. The world was wrong; and he was right. I hated this strict atmosphere and I was constantly rebelling.

I was the first one of the kids who ever dared to light a cigarette in front of my father, and he almost killed me. I'd just broke up with my girl friend—we were only in grade school—and I forgot what I was doing. As I walked into the apartment I had the cigarette in my mouth and I was lighting it. And the next thing I knew I was laying on the floor. The weed flew out of my mouth and I was so mad I grabbed it and shoved it in my mouth again. Before I could even take a drag, BOOM! My father knocked me down again. I got up on my knees with my eyes bleeding, my nose bleeding, my mouth busted. But I wouldn't give up. I still went for that cigarette. It was all smashed by now, but the last thing I remember was scraping up the loose tobacco from the floor and licking it off my fingers.

Ramiro used to be the one to open my father's church, and have everything in place. He was about four years older than me. At night when the service was over, he would be the one to close it up.

"Look at him," Dad would say to me. "He loves to go to church. He's a good boy. Why can't you be like him? Why are you so bad? What's wrong with you? You crazy?"

He used to brag about Ramiro to all the people—preachers and everybody. But one day I had my chance. I never hung around the church after the service; I'd cut out as soon as possible. And I never used to go in the back where my father's office was.

But this Sunday, I don't know why, I decided to go around the pulpit and on back to the office. As I went that way I saw the door was closed, all but just a little crack. So I peeked inside before going in. There was my brother Ramiro with his hands in the offering plate! He was taking out dimes and nickels and putting them in his coat pockets, his pants pockets, his shirt pocket. Boy! I tiptoed away, and ran as fast as I could to get my father,

"Pop, somebody's stealing outa the offering plate!"

I didn't tell him who it was, but he left the people he was talking to and was right on my tail as we ran back to the office. I let him pass me on the way and when he opened the door he saw Ramiro. POW! Dad hit him so hard that he went right up in the air, with his legs and arms flying. The coins came out of his pockets in all directions like he was exploding!

Ramiro gave me a beating after that like I'll never forget. I still got scars on my lip where he punched me. After that I used to hide everytime I'd see him alone. But I had such a desire to make it in Ramiro's eyes.

One time I was bugging him about something, and he said to me,

"Listen, you wanna hang out with us, go steal the bottle of milk off that guy."

He was trying to chase me off, to get rid of his pesty kid brother. He didn't think I'd do it.

This was a big guy, standing on the corner, waiting to cross the street. He had a newspaper he was looking at and a bottle of milk under his arm. I didn't even think about it before I ran: "If you wanna hang out with us . . . if you wanna be a tough guy, go steal that bottle of milk." I had my father's rubbers on that morning because my mom had hid my shoes on me. She had a dream that something terrible was gonna happen to me, and she didn't want me to go out of the house. She was always having premonitions, she was psychic. That's why she hid my shoes. But I found my father's rubbers, big clodhoppers, and I went out anyway, with them on.

Just before the traffic light changed I tore up to the man, snatched the bottle of milk and cut across the street, 110th and Madison. The light changed as I darted right in front of a taxicab. It plowed right over me.

My ribs were busted; my legs were busted; and they didn't think I'd live through the night. I was lying in the hospital bed, and there were two people in the room when I opened my eyes. My father and my mother's cousin were on their knees praying. They were waiting for me to die. But when I saw my father I cried out,

"Please don't hit me, Pop. Please, Pop, don't hit me."

I wasn't afraid of dying. I was afraid he was going to spank me! This was what I connected him with, even when I was barely conscious. I had a great fear of his disciplinarian ways.

That accident kept me in the hospital well over a year. And when I got out I was crippled for awhile. They didn't have no wheelchair for me so they put me in a carriage. I was about eight years old, and it was summer time. I'd sit there in the carriage on the sidewalk and yell at the guys. This was 109th Street between Park and Madison, the "block," the fighting block, where the Italians used to fight the Puerto Ricans. The big guys liked me cause they could tell me to do this or that and I would do it. If they wanted to start a fight, they'd say, "Johnny, see that guy? Go over and punch him for me." And I would do it because I knew they would back me up.

I'd won my place with them, and even that summer when I had to sit in the carriage, I was one of the boys. Guys were playing stickball and yelling, drinking wine, smoking marijuana. Cabeza, the pusher, used to come over to the carriage and say, "Johnny, hold this." And he'd give me a pack of marijuana to hold. Then these other guys would come to me and say, "OK. Gimme two." And I'd reach in the package and give them a couple of sticks. My father would be sitting right around there on the stoop. All the families would be hanging out the windows yelling and talking—making lots of noise.

I was just a little kid eight years old, and I knew already. I was "in."

It was my sister's boyfriend who gave me my first taste of marijuana. I was not quite ten at the time. I remember I went up to my house singing and carrying on. Somebody was ironing; and I walked over and picked up the ironing board and put it on top of my head. I was out of my mind! I'll never forget the beating I got when my father found out. Man! I was sick! Just kept throwing up and throwing up, falling down and getting up, and falling down again. But I can still remember laughing all the time my father was hitting me.

* * *

Father and mother had separated when I was six or seven years old. All of us kids got put away in different places. I was in and out of homes. Then my parents went back together again. We never did have much of a home life. Things were always unsettled and we felt it. I hated my father, loved him but hated him—one of those things. Dad was preaching all during these years, but he didn't much practice what he preached, so it was kind of difficult for me to look at God. I remember my grandmother on my father's side was a real Christian, but she died when I was small, and nobody I knew in New York expressed the kind of God that could have interested me.

When my parents first separated I went to live in this place that had like glass panels, like a hospital. Well, you know by now what was bound to happen sooner or later. Sure enough, one day I had a fight and I took my shoe and CRASH! right through one of those panels. Glass all over the place, and BOY! I got it.

They put me downstairs in a little dungeon. It was horrible! Just me in this dark closed-up little place. No bathroom, no nothing. I almost died in there. I was screaming and pounding and kicking against the floor. I was going mad!

Now I'd already seen death, and I'd seen killings. I seen a guy stab another guy. I seen a cop put three bullets in a man when I was just a little kid. All this didn't bother me; but when they put me in that hole and locked the door, something was wrong. They don't even put insane criminals in places like that. I could hear rats, and I thought the walls were going to cave in on me. And they left me there all day long. I was so scared.

It was my own fault that I got into messes like that. If I didn't like something it would show in me right away—my quick tongue, quick answer, quick rebellion always got me into trouble. I had a very bad temper, and I always said the wrong things, gave the wrong look.

One day I had a fight in the school. I was talking to this pretty little girl across the aisle from me—we were just kids, maybe ten years old.

"Hey, Baby, I'll meetcha after school."

She shook her head and said, "I'll tell my boyfriend."

That made me mad, "Aw! Shut up!"

"You leave me alone," she whispered.

And POW! I reached over and slapped her, right in the classroom; and she got up and told her boyfriend. And all this time the teacher's up there in front at the blackboard writing away. All of a sudden here comes this guy out of his chair and he hits me! The teacher turns around and orders us,

"All right boys, you take your seats this instant!"

But we were already tearing into each other, knocking each other around, knocking things off the desks. The kids were screaming. So the teacher comes over and she grabs me by the collar and she slaps me, too. I turned around and cursed her,

"You let me go or I'll kill you!"

She let go and I took off out the door and down the hall, with her leaning out of her room yelling after me,

"Johnny Gimenez, you come back here. I'll get you!"

I ran downstairs. I was so mad I had to do something. I looked around in the basement where the gym was and found some old newspapers and cardboard boxes. I must have been out of my mind. I rolled out the garbage can and dumped it in the middle of the floor, and threw a match in. I'm standing there watching the fire get a good start when WHAM! somebody grabs me! First they drag me up to the principal's office, then we have to go to the police station, and then when I got home—Oh! man! Dad gave me a beating that almost killed me. He did this so often, but I deserved it. He never hurt me unless I deserved it. He was such a strict disciplinarian, and I was such a bad kid!

After this my father wouldn't keep me home any longer, so they took me to the New York Shelter for Children—a kind of anti-cruelty society for humans.

3. The Street

Most of us guys grew up playing in the street. The world we knew was a kind of box. The "block" was ours—we could walk it blind. It was our nursery, our playground, our battle station.

Home was a place to sleep, and to grab some food. Most of the guys had a horror of using home for much more than that. Some called it "prison." Often growing up with an aunt, or some other relative in charge, we escaped every time we could. Fathers were often gone, many times deserted for good; and a different boyfriend every few months or years was a poor substitute — for the kids anyhow. Everybody's always moving—from Puerto Rico to Spanish Harlem, to the Bronx, to the Bowery, to the housing project. Three or four changes of address a year is just ordinary. For most of us school was a bore. It's no big thing in our world to get way up in high school and still not know how to read. Most everybody seems to get promoted whether they've learned anything or not.

Spanish Harlem is still the dope center, and we played on the stoops with junkies goofing all around us. When the government began tearing down the slum buildings, many of us Puerto Ricans and Negroes moved north to the Bronx. That's about 130th Street on the East Side, and 157th on the West. Most tourists to New York don't know nothing about the Bronx except the Cross Bronx Expressway. Riverdale's cool, man! But our world ain't that boss. Over on the East Side you get into some of the city's worst slums. And we helped keep it that way. There's old five-story brick tenements, and some new housing projects that get old overnight.

Whether the building is new or old—it don't matter. Tenants don't care how they live. Little kids use the inside hallway and the cruddy stairs for a play pen — four or five, or eight or nine, laughing and screaming, and running up and down. Junkies use the same place for a "shooting gallery." People going by on the street step inside to take a leak behind the radiator. Garbage cans are forever full and running over. Kids are always throwing stones at the cats. Clothes lines are always sagging. Women are always hanging out the windows yelling at the children,

"Andy, if you hit my Jeannie again, I'll come down and kill you!"

Kids, bored with school, sneaking into the candy store—in the hot weather squealing in the water from the fire pump. Older guys, looking for kicks, nothing to do, hanging around on the corner . . . outside the bodega, men drinking beer, playing dominoes . . . Boys in the middle of the street playing stickball . . . Bets riding on the game for forty or fifty dollars . . . Young girls parading their exciting new bodies — lounging on the stoop or leaning against the lamp post, laughing and cheering the guys on, using obscene words — which makes you really part of the "in" crowd . . . Old ladies coming out to tell the kids, "You're going to break a window"—nobody pays any attention . . . Dope fiends, goofing on the stoop, reading comic books—a "front" when you're nodding. Your head keeps going down between your knees, and you keep telling people you're reading . . . Police cruising by every half-hour in the squad car . . . Door-to-door salesmen peddling little statues of Jesus and all kinds of saints . . . Incense smoke mixing with the smell of burning beans and Puerto Rican spices.

This is the "block." Too many people, too many demands. Never enough money, little reason to try. Throw the garbage out the window, toss the beer cans in the street, use the hallway for a latrine. Who cares? Winos stagger and vomit at the curb. Ditty bops flash their switchblades. Junkies strip hubcaps, radios, batteries off parked cars. Prostitutes argue over who gets the "trick." Everybody's like crowded. Up tight! It was all just part of life for us.

4. The Gang

The center of life for us guys was the gang. It was the thing to be a gang member. That's no different from what it is any place. Kids always want to get together and make a club or a gang. It just depends on how shook-up you are as to how bad the gang gets. We weren't satisfied to play ping-pong and basketball and go to the movies. We were always looking for something with a bigger kick.

Even the names we picked used to scare us! We had the Copiens, Lightnings, Rockets, Dragons, Young Sinners, Comanches, Slicksters, Bachelors. Some of the gangs went more for status, like the Royal Knights, the Kingsmen, the Crusaders, the Viceroys, the Crowns.

Each time a boy joined the Crusaders, the leader made a slash across his arm. The new guy cut his own arm at the same time; and they would put the cuts together to mix the blood. Then each one squeezed a few drops of his blood into a shot glass of whiskey, and they'd drink it, and be real blood brothers! One of the leader's got fourteen scars on his arms.

In a gang you gotta have "heart"—that's when you're not afraid of anything or anybody. When the chips are down, you'll do anything, absolutely anything! Heart is walking up to the cop on the corner and making a grab for his pistol. Heart is taking a sawed-off shotgun and firing into a group of teenagers. Heart is taking a dare to jump down three flights of stairs.

The opposite of heart is "punking out." If one of the guys gets hurt, and you do nothing about it, you're somebody that's nothing. The gang won't have nothing to do with you. If you want them to protect you, then you got to protect them. If you don't they won't have no part of you. They won't walk around with you, 'cause they think you're gonna punk out. When it's time to fight they think you'll run.

We started this kind of gang life when we were only ten or eleven years old. We had the "cubs" and the "seniors." The seniors kind of looked out for the cubs. Sometimes there was even a gang of real little guys—maybe eight or nine year old kids. One of the reasons we started skipping school was that we just got too busy gang fighting.

The gang was our protection from the adults we didn't understand, from the unknown world that was "out there" beyond our territory. Mostly we got together because we lived close together. Some gangs were made around a common nationality—like the Italians against the Puerto Ricans. But it was more common to have a gang made up of guys from the same block or the same housing project. And most gangs had some kids from other nationalities.

Being a Negro or a Jew—that kind of stuff don't bother us. We got more personal complaints to settle—like the cat who give me a dirty look. Or the guy who called Joe a "square." Or the creep who took Tony's girl. Or the rival who kept his radio on too loud in the movie. We're all for one, and one for all.

We lived with the uneasy feeling that the other gangs out there would strike at any moment. The world outside was full of danger, but together we could take care of it. If we had to leave our own "turf" for school or work, nothing was safe. That's why one of the guys says, "I spent 22 years just walkin' round the block. Round and round and round the block."

We'd fight almost everyday. Hang out by a juke box, or in a candy store, or the park. And somebody would say, "Well, Rake got hit. We gonna have to go over there and take care of that butcher."

Everybody'd scatter to get whatever they got at home. Some would have a gun; some would have just a knife or a club. Then we'd all meet and go out together. Whoever we'd see from a rival gang, we'd jump on him.

Lots of times trouble would start because of the girls—at the swimming pool, in the park, in the candy store. Maybe a member of another gang would just touch one of our "debs," and she'd come tell us. That was all we needed. We'd grab one of their members; they'd grab one of ours. Then there'd be a big war council and we'd send a message to tell them, "We're gonna fight."

That's what the war counselor does—he goes into enemy territory and declares war. Usually the club would be fair and let the guy walk out after he brought the message. Most of the time there'd be other representatives nearby who could close in immediately if he was up tight.

We used to have some good fights—almost every week we'd be in one of the papers. Somebody got killed over there. Somebody got shot over here. When you're fighting, it isn't frightening. You're just doing it, you're not thinking about what might happen. After it's all over and you have a party someplace, you talk about it. Then your mind starts thinking—this coulda happened. And you remember the person who really got hurt and you put yourself in his place. But you only think like that after you get back and it's all over.

We never knew no different. This is the way the world is, we thought. Tough. They's always going to be gangs. Always going to be fighting. Always people going to get killed. That's life.

Still way down inside we were always wondering. Maybe there's something somewhere that can stop the hungry feeling. So we hung out by the juke box and made our gangs and sharpened our knives. And we didn't even know that 99% of the kids in New York City were different. Oh, they were searching too; but they did it by watching TV and listening to Elvis Presley and studying their lessons. We weren't always fighting — lots of times we weren't doing nothing but sitting around waiting for something to happen.

Different types of cliques we had. We used to have dances in the PAL center. That's the Police Athletic League, 156th Street and Fox Street. It was a Center with a poolroom and basketball. Different teachers and coaches were there to teach us all kinds of things. We used to hold dances there every Friday night. It was a good place to go, but we did things on the sneak anyway. Really the only thing legal was the place — everything else we'd do on the sneak — like smoke marijuana. We'd go outside, take a walk around, smoke a "joint," drink some beer. Then we'd come back upstairs to the dance. You see, for us it was a good life. We enjoyed it. It was the thing to do.

Now the gang fighting has pretty much played out in New York—everybody's using drugs. Wherever we were, we kept up the search for some magic answer—looking for a way to get the pain out of life, for a way to be a real man. Trying and failing, trying and failing. Gang fighting filled in for awhile, but it was just a stage. Smoking pot seemed a good way for some of us to escape the real world that hurt so much. The law locked us up to keep us out of the way. But we kept on looking for the doorway into a world where nothing could bother us. Along with the gangs and the marijuana came the girls. And this was the biggest mystery of all for some of us!

5. The Girls

When I was 13 I ran away from Children's Village—walked about 25 miles back to New York City. I didn't want to go home because I knew they'd look there first for me. It was maybe three or four o'clock in the afternoon when I turned into this apartment building on 104th Street, and went up to the roof to lay down. About six o'clock I woke up hungry. I knew the milk man was coming around, so I started downstairs to get me some milk. As I was going down, there was a lady coming out one of the doors, and as I kept walking I heard her say,

"Johnny?"

When I turned around I just looked at her.

"Don't you know me?" she asked. "My name is Rita. I'm a friend of your sister's. I remember you from 109th Street."

We struck up a conversation. She could see I was dirty, so she asked where I come from, and I told her I been up on the roof. It came out later that I had run away from this home, so she invited me into her house to give me something to eat.

"Where ya gonna stay?" she asked.

"I dunno."

"If you want to stay here you can—till you find some place to go."

So I did. I ate like a hog and then went to sleep and I slept for hours and hours. She was attractive, about 30 years old, and very good to me. I didn't know it then but she was a prostitute. It wouldn't have mattered to me anyway 'cause it was the most common thing in our neighborhood. After about three or four days, she and I became intimate. She wasn't a street walker; she knew the right people. She had her own phone book—went by appointment to her customers.

She drove me everywhere. Guys knew me, and they knew her. That's where I got the nickname, "Johnny Pimp." A prostitute needs a man to take care of her—to see that she gets her money, and doesn't get abused by the "trick." It would be better for her if she didn't need him, because she really can't use him sexually. She just needs the protection he can give her.

When you get involved in this life one thing leads to another. You go to a dance, you meet this girl. She hustles. She needs an old man. Usually the women were much older than I. I left Rita because I got arrested.

I'm not proud of it; but since then I've had a lot of affairs, a lot of women, fathered a lot of children. Women are important to us. In fact, some of the doctors and psychiatrists who are making all kinds of studies of addicts think that understanding sex is perhaps the biggest single problem in narcotics addiction.

A lot of us grew up in a private world which was made up largely of women—mothers, aunts, grandmother, sisters. Sure, some of us did have fathers but most of the guys just took it as part of life to have a father come and go, or disappear completely. Women were the backbone. Maybe guns and knives and beer and dope and tattoos and filthy talk all made us feel big, rough, male. Love? That was woman stuff. Men had to be brutal, we thought. Learning how to be a man wasn't easy in our world. Some guys would get up their courage and approach some swinging chick. Up on the roof with her, he'd want so much to be a man, but somehow he couldn't. One of the guys went home after that kind of deal and cried himself to sleep. After that he changed—he had to prove he was tough somehow, so he threw stones at the windows in the apartments, and scratched shiny cars, and carried a switchblade. Then he started smoking pot — you see, when you're "high" you're just a quiet nothing. It don't matter who you are or what you're supposed to do.

Sex was very confusing but very common. In our neighborhod it was in the raw. It was ugly, and it was physical all the way. Everything was sex—the curse words implied the deep-down "gut" kind of sex.

Little kids, playing house in the back yards go through all the motions. I was a tiny kid when I was playing Daddy and Mommy with this girl who's one of the biggest pushers in the Bronx today. It was nothing really, but we acted it all out. You learn fast; there's no innocent kids in our neighborhood. They're grown up before they have a chance to be a child, because of the things they see. In the crowded apartments, there's not much private; and what they miss there they pick up from the examples of older kids—on the rooftops, in the park. One kid will watch and describe everything that happens—don't leave nothing undone.

By the time you're in junior high school you never think of going out with a girl more than twice unless she wants to have a full sex relationship with you. All the gang members got their own deb. It's just that way. I never went with a girl—maybe one that I can remember—that I didn't do it with. Girls fell kind of into three groups: the lays, the in-betweens, and the debs. A "lay" was just a way of relieving sex tensions—we used her pretty bad. An "in-between' got good treatment sometime, but not always. A "deb" was somebody we wanted to be seen with, somebody we'd fight for and protect, no matter what happened to us.

All three kinds got pregnant now and then, and we thought we were really men if we could say, "I got a son" or a "daughter." We were usually proud, not disturbed, if we succeeded in getting a girl pregnant. So we didn't even try to be careful, and lots of girls worried a great deal about what would happen to them, but they usually went along anyway.

If she did get pregnant, and the family made it rough for us, or we got charged with rape, we would do the decent thing and marry her. Looking back at the trail of broken marriages, though, I'm not sure that's always the best answer for either the girl or the guy.

It was rough for the girls, sometimes filthy. I remember times when we used to run down the street and there'd be a girl walking along minding her own business. We'd just sweep her up; everybody would grab a different part of her and keep right on running, carrying her along with us. (There was one guy in our neighborhood we called Macky "Body-snatcher.") Ten, maybe fifteen, guys would take her up on the roof, and they'd line up, one right after another.

One girl it happened to threw herself off the roof. She didn't die, but her body's all twisted, paralyzed. It all started because she wanted to go with this one guy she liked. She was a pretty little girl, only about 16, but she was already a woman; she'd had relations with guys. Now she wanted to go with just one guy. But he called his friends, about seven guys, and they lined up and took turns with her. When they were finished she just stumbled over to the edge of the roof and dropped to the sidewalk five floors down. That's only one case.

They tried to do that once with a girl I used to go with. She and I were doing it on the roof, just her and me—she was my deb. Then my cousin came upstairs and said,

"Johnny, come on down, man. There's a rumble!"

So I kissed her and told her, "Wait, I'll see you later."

When I ran down, these guys came up through the other building and got onto the roof where she was. But you know, I sensed something. I was going downstairs, when all of a sudden I turned around and was running back up. I had a pistol too. When I got there they had her and they were getting ready, but they hadn't done anything yet.

I put the pistol to this guy's head, "Get offa there, you creep, or I'll kill ya."

I was gonna kill him too, and he knew it.

"Aw, we're just kiddin', man!" But they cut out, fast.

I had a deep feeling for this girl. One time we were going to commit suicide together—going to throw ourselves off the roof. We were just kids in our early teens. I used to knock her around; she was one of those girls that likes to get hit. We'd been smoking marijuana, and then she started arguing about having a baby. She never did have no baby, but she was always afraid she would. So we battled till I was out of my mind, and I said,

"Let's end it. It's no use. Let's just kill ourselves."

She agreed—we couldn't get along together, but we didn't want to go on without each other. There were a lot of things involved. So we walked over to the edge of the roof. Then she backed out. I was going to go; I would have gone through with it.

I did almost get killed because of this same girl. Somebody came to me and said,

"Johnny, they beat up your girl!"

I knew right away that she had started it, 'cause she was that way. And I could just hear her,

"Well, my boy friend, Johnny, he's rough, man!"

So I went down there to check it out. I had a derringer, and I hit this guy with it. Then I found out it was her fault—she called him a "creep." About two days later, her and me was coming into the block when we saw about fifteen of their gang. I didn't have a chance to run and I didn't have my gun with me. I just told them, "Keep goin'!" I could see they had four guns on us.

"OK, man. Why did ya hit this guy? Tell us."

"I hit him because he hit my ol' lady."

"Man! do you know she came around here and she started talking big, and she called him a creep? Do you know that? Suppose I hit her again?"

"You do, and I'll punch you in the mouth."

Out of the corner of my eye I saw my boys coming — with three sawed-off shotguns. I knew they'd take care of us now, so I wasn't afraid.

"You hurt her and I'll punch you in the mouth. Hear?"

"Yeah? Well I'll kill ya!"

"So you kill me?"

"Then tomorrow she'll be with somebody else."

"That's tomorrow. As long as she's my girl nobody touches her."

"Well, you better not let her do it again, or we'll wash ya!"

They had started backing away when they seen the Barons there. They knew we'd shoot—even though we often shot away from people rather than at them.

Things got even more confusing for us guys as we got more hooked. Some time later in the Bronx my friend Duke and I were with this Jewish group. We enjoyed parties, and we liked girls.

One day we went to cop some pills, and we were all up on the rooftop getting high. There were a couple of girls—real swingers, and my friend Duke was very forward. He thought a lot of himself—thought no girl could resist him.

He was sitting there talking with this girl. You know, you right away team up. And Duke must of "hit on her," as we say.

"Look, Baby," I heard him say, "Let's make it."

And the girl started laughing and laughing and laughing. We all turned around and she says,

"Dig this, gang! Hey, dig this square. He's talkin' about *sex*."

Like it was the most hilarious thing. Everybody started laughing and Duke turned red and almost cried, he was so embarrassed. I didn't see what was so funny then. But later I learned this is the kind of thing that happens when you're on dope. For this guy to come out in the middle of a "horse party" and talk about going off some place alone—this was crazy!

I found out later. For three months I slept in the same bed with a woman and never once touched her. We'd use the same dope, the same bag, the same spike. But we never once, not even held hands. Dope was our everything.

* * *

Sex was something anybody could buy, or make arrangements for, in our neighborhood. About 1:30 any afternoon you could see the girls, the hustlers, standing on the corner. They're usually between 18 and 35 years old, and some of them look like pigs. Many are addicts and this is their way of supporting a big habit.

They don't bother much with makeup and their hair don't look too good; some aren't even clean. When it's cold they stand around in leotards and hand-me-down coats, maybe a scarf around their heads, or a funny little woolen cap with ear flaps. Boots that are broken down, coffee stains on their jackets, burnt spots from cigarettes, make a pretty repulsive picture. Some are yawning 'cause they're sick and they haven't turned a trick yet to get that wake-up shot.

One of the girls sees a trick coming down the street — one of her favorites. She goes to approach him, but another girl does too. They are hungry; they both want this money for that fix. They're not interested in sex, only in the money which they can get through selling their bodies over and over again.

The first girl says, "Five dollars."

The other one puts her price at "Four-fifty."

The first counters with "Four."

And from there they go down, further degrading themselves. This is the competition they face constantly with each other. The man finally goes with the cheapest one—perhaps for three dollars.

A hustler's always in dirty water. When a girl uses drugs it's really bad; she'll just keep going and going and going. And she very often has to turn to prostitution to earn enough money. You look at the girls on the street, and it ain't easy to have respect for them.

I knew a girl from our block who was a prostitute for 16 years, and on dope all that time. Her father died when she was six, and her mother went on welfare. Before she was fourteen she discovered she could get ten or fifteen dollars real easy if she'd go across the hall to the landlord's apartment and just let him touch her breasts. With the money she'd buy food for her mother and the younger children. When she'd walk in to the flat with shopping bags full of groceries her mother would wonder where she got it, but she would lie about where she'd been and how she'd earned it.

I heard her say in later years, "If I ever have a daughter, I'll sit her down and tell her the facts of life. Nobody ever informed me. I didn't know anything." She was raped at 14.

Two years later she met a guy 37 years old and was real gone on him. That's when she started hustling—for him. He took care of her for seven years, pushed narcotics, and she had all the dope she could use. She was always high.

"I couldn't go to bed with a guy unless I was high on stuff," she says. "I was so ashamed—all the time I was hustling. I might go to bed twenty times in a night—it was just 1-2-3 that's all, but I had to be high 'cause I felt so bad if I wasn't. It went against my nature."

We didn't know what love was. One of the boys would say, "When you love persons you take care of them. I never took care of my wife. Oh, I would take her out to dine. I was proud of her, but I would be five or six days out of my house. If she would be jealous when I came back I would just hold up my fist and she'd straighten out."

We needed somebody who was ours—somebody to speak with, to share with. Living with prostitutes, common-law relationships, early or sudden marriages satisfied little of the deep need that drove us on in our search for something—we weren't quite sure what. Something "cool," something swinging, something that could make us feel big, something that wouldn't go away, but would stay with us forever and ever and ever.

But our relationships with women—good or bad, couldn't be more than part of the answer. The more involved we got with narcotics, the more we were out to get. We didn't want that girl to get too close; we just wanted to be sure of a good bargain.

In the process we did find little pieces of help—some of us. Other times we failed miserably. And the failures led us on to deaden the suffering of the beatings we took in our most intimate thoughts. Dope was easily in our reach and we grabbed for its living death.

6. The Jails —The Hospitals

More than any other time, a junkie needs help right after he comes out of jail, or out of the hospital. There's something about the way they do everything for you that can take the place of drugs. You don't need to think for yourself; you don't have to decide anything. You just do what they tell you to do. Then BOOM! all of a sudden you're outside again, and you don't know where to go, or what to do. And it's too much. So you run for the needle.

When I was in the Reformatory I didn't want to use dope. I wrote home, "Never again!" But I hadn't been back in New York an hour when my nose started to run, my eyes started to tear, I started dry-heaving, shaking, sweating. I had sold my freedom of choice. All the good things in life that the "squares" go for were unimportant now, and out of reach. Family, education, travel, entertainment, business—they all fell out. That little bag of bitter powder ruled my life. Heroin—the garbage from morphine and five times more addictive—was my god.

Many people try to help. Medical people are spending millions of dollars to figure us junkies out. Prison staffs keep studying, but they have few of the reasons,. or the answers. My family suffered endlessly trying to help me get free. They gave and gave and gave till they had little left of themselves or their possessions. And what they didn't give, I took before they had a chance to protect it.

Every addict's got his family up tight. A habit is no private hell. means deathly sickness, horrible terrors.

You wouldn't believe how we abused them and humiliated them over and over and over again. How we stole from them till there was nothing left to steal. You know, people can take just so much, even when they love you. Husbands, wives, mothers and fathers every day risk their lives to try to help us. And if they finally give out, don't you be too hard on them. You'd give out too. A habit's the worst kind of hell for those you love.

My family was always hoping when I got out of jail, or the hospital, that I was gonna stay clean. So, when I fell on the needle again as soon as I was outside—in copping distance, things were really bad for them. Hope comes and goes for them.

Normal people couldn't understand how that numbness could take away our need for sex or for personality. When we were sick for dope we could look at that shot and say, "You're my mother, you're my father, you're my lover. You're everything I ever want in life. And you better get me high!"

* * *

Your first time in jail is rough. Here you are in prison—with bars! You only seen it in movies before. Now you hear the doors go CLANG! CLANG! And you hear some of the inmates gnashing their teeth. And some of them are screaming and yelling,

"I'm gonna break your head open when I get outa this cell tomorrow morning."

Somebody else is cursing, and you get scared! Man! These guys have been in jail before. One loud mouth calls out,

"Hey, Up in B-5?"

And you yell back, "Whad'ya want?"

"You're a punk, yeah?"

"So? You are too, ya know!"

"Yeah? Well, we'll see when we come out. We're gonna fight."

When you come out, he gives you a rap. You give him a rap. He gives you another rap, until the cop comes over and raps you both. It's terrible and you're really scared. But you gotta put up a front. Something's whispering inside: "Wow! What did I get into?" You see everybody in there like wild animals. And everyone is observing, but they're all fronting. They don't want to show anyone they're cowards. But they watch you and they boast,

"I use drugs."

"Yeah, I steal a car."

Then you may get some kid who cracks up while he's in there. Too much.

The worst thing about going to jail when you're hooked is the kick. We call kicking a habit "cold turkey." It's a phrase that has little meaning to the average person. But to the drug addict "cold turkey"

It means eyes running water like you're crying. It means thick saliva and continual heaving all the time. It means legs and arms that won't stop trembling. It means bones that ache and a stomach torn by unbearable pains. It means nerves coming alive so your whole body feels like it's crawling with bugs. It means your sense of smell is distorted so everything smells bad. It means banging your head against the wall or on the floor. It means panting and shivering and sweating and total exhaustion. It means you can't eat or sleep. It means the bare loneliness of a jail cell together with the indifference or brutality of the police officer in charge. Some of the officers you meet are real nice. Others must just hate themselves. You can't even look at them without them growling, "What're ya lookin' at?"

People are people though. If anyone functions at all normally they're gonna feel something for you. The officer may look at you and say,

"Aaaa! Dirty, filthy dope fiend!" But he can't dismiss it; he thinks about it.

They take you in and they search you and get all your drugs and they throw you in the cell. But you can hear them talking:

"Why do they use drugs?"

"Can't they see what it's doing to them?"

"Yeah, I know this kid. He's a neighbor of mine. He's a drug addict too. I hate them."

* * *

But jail ain't the only cage we get locked into. We're always locked like an animal in a cage, when we're hooked. Wild. Tense. Restless. Our skin's a cage, and we're desperate to get out. But the only key we got is drugs. We just got to have that shot to unlock the cage we're in.

So we steal. Or we lie. Or we cheat. So we can shoot dope, and get out of the cage. But the cage is always there. You're always like walking the street that's got no way out. And you bump into yourself, and your parents, and your children, and your wife—until you're one big hurt all over. And they are too!

Like the day I came home from Auburn Prison. I was four years behind bars. Four long years without any drugs. And while I was there I said over and over again,

"I'm never gonna stick that spike in my vein again! Never! I ain't gonna be a dirty filthy junkie. I ain't gonna be a criminal. I ain't gonna be hated by society!"

The day I walked out of that jail was beautiful. I was clean. I was free. I was healthy. And I was going home. A shiny new world lay out there in front of me. As I got on the bus I thought, "My children will be grown . . . my mother will have the bed all made up with fresh sheets for me . . . the house will smell of rice and beans cooking . . . we'll hug each other . . . and cry and laugh and talk."

The 300 miles between Auburn and the Bronx couldn't go too fast. I remember looking at the farms and the little towns. I thought about the fathers playing with their children in the yard together, walking to the store, and praying after they turned out the lights.

And I thought of the girl I married when she was just 13 . . . and the disappointment I brought her. I thought about how she took all she could and then gave up and left me.

"I wanna see her," my heart cried inside of me. "I love you, Gina! I wanna get a groovy pad for you and me and the kids! I want us to be a real family!"

But as I thought of them and of the Bronx, and the streets that I walked so many days and nights — sometimes high and silly, other times sick and desperate — something crazy began to happen to me.

My mind began to see bags, and needles, and cookers. And I seen the dope bubbling up in the cooker. And the whole wild picture sat there before my eyes—the farms and houses, and people all began to blur into one big bubbling bottle cap full of heroin. I could see it so plainly that I began to get "sick." My nose began to run. My eyes began to tear. And I got those awful pains in my stomach like I never stopped using dope for those four long years. I coughed and gagged, and people turned around and frowned at me.

By the time the bus pulled into the Port Authority Bus station at Eighth Avenue and 40th Street I was an addict in agony. I jumped off the bus and grabbed a cab. It hit every red light between Downtown and 150th Street. The streets of the Bronx looked the same. The dealers were still there on the stoops. And it wasn't hard at all. In a very few minutes I bought a bag of heroin and headed for a basement. That quickening and desire—almost like an elation, made me tremble as I got the drug in the cooler. I was nervous—sweating and shivering until I finally stuck the spike in my vein. It was like an orgasm—and I felt so good. Now I was at peace with the world.

And . . . I was a normal animal again.

* * *

If it weren't for the hospitals and jails, most junkies would probably die. We go to the hospitals to rest and to clean up physically so we can go out again and hustle a little better. The same guys come in and out. Some of them must have been there seventy times! But they don't find much of an answer. The doctors keep giving you medicine; they don't give you much hope. But you do get some sleep, and put on some weight.

Most of us were in Riverside Hospital at one time or another. It was out in the East River, and New York State was pretty determined to make it a success They started it in 1952 and we used to have to sign this thing in order to get in. This meant we were under their responsibility, and they could do anything they wanted with us. It was supposed to take in kids between 16 and 21 years of age. They even had a public school out there on North Brother's Island.

A lot of guys who came in smuggled dope with them. Some of them put it in a rubber finger and tied it shut, and then swallowed it. After they got settled, they would vomit it up or let it pass through the stool. Some drugs were floated to the island in sealed cans. They even say some parents brought in drugs to their children on visiting days.

In 1958 the New York Health Department began to check up on what good was being done at Riverside. They studied 247 patients who had been admitted to Riverside for the first time during 1955. They found out that 11 were dead. Only 19% were found outside of a prison or a hospital. 63% were psychiatric problems. Of those who had gone to Riverside without police records, 52% had gotten into trouble with the law. 65% who were familiar cases to the police had gotten new "beefs"; 51% of all the busts were for narcotics possession. 95% admitted they'd gone back to narcotics after they got out and were hooked.

Eventually Riverside Hospital was closed down. The report read: "Any organized program dealing with the problem of drug addiction is faced with the historical fact that no therapeutic success of any significance has ever been recorded." Today the state and city health authorities are looking for other ways.

7. Today . . . Any Way

When my family couldn't take it any longer and told me to get out I would take to the rooftops or the basements. That's how a junkie lives when the door at home is closed to him. The superintendent in an apartment building may let you hide out in a dark corner of the cellar. Or you may just walk into a building like you was going into your own house, and you go all the way up the stairs. There's usually a landing at the top with a skylight overhead, and a door that opens outside on the roof. At least it's a ceiling over your head, and if nobody else has claimed this spot, and the janitor doesn't stop you on the way in, you can try to make it home for a little while. You'll take some newspapers or you'll find a big cardboard carton and flatten it out, to keep you from the cold hard marble floor.

You usually don't have a blanket, so you just lie down with your clothes on. If you're lucky you may have found an extra pair of pants you can sleep in. When you're high you'll be comfortable for the night, except that you got to always keep watching any time you hear any kind of noise. You're kind of afraid 'cause you know if a policeman comes, you'll go to jail.

About 7:30 in the morning you hear the "super" sweeping, and then you hear the kids going off to school. First thing when you open your eyes you got to reach for your "works"—eye dropper, needle, and bottle top or spoon. That's the wake up shot so you can get straight enough to think, "What am I going to do today?" From the time the spike goes into your vein until the fix wears off, you got to scheme, "How can I get the bread—that's money—for the next shot?" Always figuring a new angle for a lucky break. Looking for another way to get ahead.

If you find a bathroom to wash up it's all right; if you don't it's all right. You really don't care. You knock on a door, and if somebody's there you make up a story. Maybe you tell them you're looking for somebody; it doesn't matter if you give out a wrong name 'cause actually the person don't remember the names of all the people in the building. If nobody answers, you may take a knife and try to open the lock. Or you may go downstairs, and around to the barber shop where they let you use their bathroom to wash up and shave and comb your hair. Now you can go out and look normal.

There are different ways of going about the "work" of the morning. A "booster"—if he had nothing in his pocket—his mind would remember something he saw yesterday that he could steal. He goes to this shop, and while the manager is busy with a customer, he picks up this phonograph and goes out onto the street with it under his arm. He heads for the house of a "fence" who knows him and he asks,

"Can you hold this for me till I do something? It belongs to my mother."

This way he'll certainly give you the money because this is just to pawn it, to hold it till you get the money. If you ask him for $15 or $20, he'll put it down a little; they always do. But he'll give you cash. You probably have to boost five times the amount you're going to need in stolen goods, because the fence will only give you one-fifth the true value of the loot. Then after you haggle forever with the fence, you take your money and head over to the avenue to start hunting for a connection — the pusher, the dealer who has junk for sale. Good stuff—"dynamite," not "garbage." If the dealer isn't there you start complaining,

"This creep doesn't come. I got the money and I'm sick and I ain't gonna cop from this guy here because his stuff is no good."

You always try and wait for the best connection, so you can be sure of your fix. Many times when he does come he don't got no more dope. Sometimes you got to go over to his apartment. But that's no good, 'cause he don't want to open the door. And if he does, you have to get it and run away fast before anybody sees him dealing. Lots of times he won't sell it. "Copping" is a risky business. You know "the man" is watching you, so you play it real cool.

Maybe the pusher's in the candy store or the luncheonette. It's better that way. You just drop your money on the floor; then he drops the bag. Then if you got more money you drop it, and when you stoop down to pick it up you pick up your beautiful little bag of junk too. That way it's more comfortable to both of you. That way, even if the cop would see, he couldn't say nothing.

The sickness gets worse once you have the stuff in your hands 'cause you're anxious. Your eyes water, you start to sweat, you begin to feel cold and achy like you were coming down with a bad case of the flu. You're weak and irritable, and you wish all these creeps would quit getting in your way. You head back to your rooftop, where you hid your set of works before you left. On the roof you're scared because if the cop comes now you'll have to throw everything away. It's getting caught with the junk or the works on us that's the "beef."

You take your belt and tie it around your arm; you pull it tight and your veins come up. You're tense, nervous, thinking what would have happened if your works had been gone, if the dealer hadn't come, if the cop seen you take the phonograph. You rip open the little glassine bag and empty the powder into the bottle cap. Then you put some water in and light a match under the mixture. It's kind of a ceremony, watching the stuff bubble up in the "cooker"; you stir it with the needle and dropper and then pull it up in the eye dropper and set the needle. This is the moment you live for—the shooting up, the taking off. Stick it in your vein and squeeze! And from the pit of your stomach you can feel the sensation spreading all through you — slowly. And for that moment, you are like in ecstasy. You're not in need of anything for that one moment. And as you feel this goodness take over, you start playing with your blood—that's a kick. You "boot" it awhile. Maybe you reach out and light a cigarette while the needle is still in your arm. A slow drag and this combination makes real fulfillment. You play with the blood and you breathe in the smoke and you start nodding over the needle. You're all drowsy and you don't care now if the cop comes or not. Nothing matters. Nothing at all.

A whole hour may go by before the thought begins to slip into your mind, "I'm high now, but I need some more money to get high again later on!" You just get "straight" for a couple of hours and then you need some more stuff in your body. After you take the spike out of your arm, you take everything apart and clean the dropper and the needle in a glass of water. You may suck the needle with your mouth to see if it's unclogged, and then you wrap it all up in a piece of paper and hide it again. You're not going to hide it in the same place because somebody might have been watching before. Sometimes you just sit there and wish you had a place to go, or someone to speak with. Time really goes by and you don't do nothing.

Maybe you go around and set your rooftop real clean, pick up all the papers. And the next thing is to go downstairs, and while you're walking out in the street, you try to recover in your mind what to do next. You could go over to the apartments, knock on doors. If there was nobody home, you'd use your screwdriver to break the door open so you could go in and take a TV or a phonograph, or search for money. If you don't find nothing you look in the cars, and if you see anything inside you break the window. If you don't see nothing in the cars then you go over and try to sneak from a store again. Maybe you boost in the "5 and 10" this time. Just trying to make money for the next shot.

In New York City alone junkies hustle up $700,000 a day to stay high. That makes a pretty busy day for an addict on the street. They ain't hardly time to keep even. What a stupid way to live! Staying up most of the night to take care of your habit. When you do go to sleep, you have nightmares—wake up cold, sweating. Your heart beats like someone was chasing you. Then if you can't go back to sleep, you cook up a little more stuff and get high again. Then everything's all warm and quiet.

If it's "garbage" I would cry with frustration, "That dirty punk!" Or, I might laugh. The whole crazy routine looks so ridiculous sometimes we gotta laugh in spite of our sickness. All we could do anyway was start out all over again and hope for better luck next time.

Heroin is the most inflated stuff in the world. The little peasants who grow it get eighty cents a day, and starve. Junkies who buy it pay five dollars a bag, and die! We use over a ton of heroin every year in the United States. Costs $300 million a ton. That's 250 times as expensive as gold! And it's all imported. All illegal.

When you got a big habit—"an oil burner"—it may cost you up to $100 a day. And you're stuck with it!

Dead to everything but "junk." Hypnotized by the blood going up and down in the dropper. Goofing on the same block year after year. Staring at the coffee stain on my pants for hours on end. Roused to hustling only when the junk runs out. It's get that money or else! We been taught over and over again what happens when we don't get it.

Nothing else matters. How we got it doesn't matter. Who we hurt in the deal. We couldn't care less. We wear out the love of relatives and friends, and they try to forget we ever existed. We're driven day and night by our need. We cling to each other in our weakness, in our crime, so we won't be completely and forever alone.

We get even with the world that's always in our way by taking whatever we can use from our neighbors, or from the strangers who enter our block. We learn how to use stick-ups, armed robberies, prostitution, forgery, muggings, shoplifting, extortion, short-change, scalpings, flim-flam. They're all part of a day's work. We got to have money for that junk we can't live without. And in getting it, we often get "busted" and thrown in jail.

* * *

I remember one day when I was back at my house on Fox Street. My sister Donna had been converted in the biggest Spanish church in the Bronx. "John 3:16" they call it—it's still there. Anyway, she thought it was time I got converted too, so she told me,

"Johnny, if you go to church tonight, I'll give you ten dollars."

I'd stopped going to church when we were little kids but to me ten dollars was ten pills! So I told my friend Duke, "Look, gimme a coupla pills till tonight."

"No, man."

"Look, gimme a pill! 'Cause my sister — she's gonna gimme ten dollars tonight if we go to church."

Duke gave me the pill, and that night he went with me to church. We sat down near the back across the aisle from Donna. They sang and they made a lot of noise; and we're waiting and waiting.

"Baloney!" I thought, "this jumping around is crazy." I didn't like it.

When the message was over, the preacher began making an altar call; I knew what that was all about. I was positive my sister had told that man all about me.

"Now you know you're in sin. You're a trouble maker. You know all this and you're goin' to hell."

I was sure she had informed on me. And the more he talked, the more I put my head down.

"Better come to God tonight. You don't know. If you walk outa here tonight you might drop dead."

I looked to the side and my sister was looking right at me. She had the ten dollar bill in her hand, and she wiggled it and pointed with the other hand at the altar. I got the message: You better go up there, Johnny, or you don't get the ten dollars.

I looked at Duke and he hit me: "Go. Go."

So I stepped out in the aisle and walked all the way down to the altar. Duke didn't. He was killed within the year. I believe with all my heart that some kind of stamp was put on me that night. My mind often goes back to that incident.

I felt funny when I got on my knees. Felt like a million people jumped on me and started praying over me. I heard my sister screaming, "Lord, save him!" Man! I just wanted to get outa there. I was getting sick for dope—sweating, and my eyes were running with tears. And all these people had their hands on me and I wished they'd get away and leave me alone.

Finally my sister gave me the ten dollars, and I found Duke and we went out and bought ten pills right away—these were capsules and we'd take the powder out and cook it up with water. I gave him one pill. Then I put three in the cooker—the most I had ever taken before was two at a time. We were up on Duke's roof on Simpson Street—today it's one of the biggest dope centers. Duke kept telling me,

"Johnny, don't take so much!"

But I was twisted. I didn't listen to him. I shot it all in my vein.

The next thing I knew Duke was slapping my face and walking me around in the hall. If it hadn't been for Duke I'd a gone on out. I took an OD, and fell down the steps. Duke picked me up and kept moving me around till I came to; he got me home too. Duke and I were tight. He was my buddy, and I like to died when he got killed by the cops a year later.

8. The Stuff

The traffic in "junk" is an immense international scandal. Beating it is something like trying to empty the sea with a little spoon.

It begins in the fields of modest peasants who have grown opium poppies as a cash crop for centuries, and it dives underground almost immediately. Theoretically, in Turkey, for instance, all raw opium must be sold to a government monopoly; but the rules don't work. Dealing with a smuggler often will double a peasant's earnings — which, even at that increase, will never make him rich. His problem is chiefly one of survival.

The smugglers who move opium across the Near East borders are a rugged lot who are little concerned with customs regulations. They do battle regularly with border patrols, and their life expectancy is not very great. In places like Syria, Lebanon and Turkey, smuggling is sometimes a way of making a living passed on from father to son.

If the opium is bound for the United States to become heroin, the smugglers convert it to a morphine base, mainly to reduce bulk. This can be done in an old oil drum over a slow fire in the desert. A hundred kilos of opium reduces to ten kilos of morphine powder which is poured into sacks and moved on to Europe to be purified and converted into heroin.

Accomplished underworld Corsicans and various Italian racketeers with allies in America long fought for the smuggling rights between the Near East and the United States. Heroin manufacture was still legal in Italy after World War II, but Bureau of Narcotics investigations and United Nations intervention eventually resulted in the banning of all heroin production in Italy. Today the experienced Corsicans succeed in buying morphine base in Beirut and Istanbul, smuggling it along several routes into Europe, where it goes into a tedious laboratory conversion process in Paris, Marseilles, and other cities.

Between France and the United States there are three main routes: direct to New York; via Canada; and via Mexico. The most effective method employed at this stage has been the use of diplomatic couriers, who do not have to undergo customs inspection; however, there are many cunning devices constantly used to beat the highly developed inspections system at all border points. Junk filters in through the piers and airports and truck routes despite the relentless attempts of customs officials and narcotics agents — imbedded in canned food, in engines of airliners, jammed behind steel plates of ships' hulks, in automobile headlights and skillfully contrived secret compartments, in false bottoms of immigrant luggage, in underclothing, in corpses being returned to relatives, and within the human body.

New York is the hub of the narcotic distribution system. Perhaps no more than a half-dozen importers direct the main traffic. Out of New York it moves on to Chicago, Detroit, Washington, Philadelphia, Cleveland. It is impossible to say how much profit is made on these transactions, but it has to be sizable to be worth the great risks involved. Some of the third and fourth generation junk dealers are moving out of the old Italian neighborhoods and out of the narcotics racket, finding a distaste for the increasing heat in the business.

Leading importers rarely even see the narcotics they buy. This is done by subordinates. The high-up gives advice and lays out cash; the subordinate does the lugging and the hustling. It is a demanding business as well as a dangerous one. These subordinates must test everything to be sure the imported product maintains a high quality; junkies tend to deal only with pushers who have the best stuff.

Customers at this stage are spread throughout the city, and they, too, must work with extreme caution. One of them may set up a base of operations in a rented apartment. Here he may have three or four helpers sitting around a table. One mixes the heroin with milk sugar or quinine; another spoons it into little glassine bags (like stamp collectors use); another folds and tapes them shut. If the workers are not addicts, they wear masks to prevent addiction from inhaling the dust.

At this level the junk business becomes chaotic. More and more people become involved in the international criminal trade as the tiny packets hit the street. Most of them are addicts. They buy what they can, use what they need, and sell the rest. Ultimately the police will catch up with all of them. In New York a man needs as little as $25 to get started—that buys half a load. And that's where I came in.

9. The Pusher

Every addict is a potential pusher 'cause when he can push dope off on somebody else, it gives him more money for his own habit. Junkie pushers are their own best dope customers, 'cause when they're pushing they use up a good amount of stuff. The pushers who are not on dope you never see—they're the big ones, the junk higher-ups. I had a couple good connections in my time.

Davy was a Jewish boy. His father was a "cooker"—a tester who finds out how pure the imported heroin is before it gets distributed to dealers. He had an important job. Davy dug me 'cause I always came right. I'd been working for him a few months, and I never came short—always had the right money. Sometimes I even had extra for an advance. If he give me an ounce for $100, BOOM-BOOM! I'd have the $100 plus $50 more for the next one. I was always ahead of the game with him and he dug it. So one day he come to see me with a shoe box.

I almost died! There was 32 ounces of heroin inside! He had two rooms where he kept stuff, and the "bulls" had busted one of them. He was afraid to stay in his place anymore, so he brought me the shoe box to hold and to sell what I could from it. For every ounce I sold I gave him $100. Out of an ounce I'd get 150 bags to sell for five dollars each. So I was making more than five times my money.

When I was selling "weight" (half an ounce or an ounce at a time), rather than bags, I'd deal with other connections. A guy would call and I'd make the meet with him—in a train station, on a subway. He'd give me the money; I'd give him the weight.

In a luncheonette I would be sitting at the counter drinking coffee, and I'd have the stuff on me. I take out an empty cigarette pack and put it in there. When a certain guy comes, he'll sit next to me. This is pre-arranged; he's ordered half a load. I shoot the pack down next to my feet, not too far. When he passes the money to me I look down. He sees the pack on the floor, picks it up, finishes his coffee and goes.

In a bad situation I would come into a restaurant and all the addicts were waiting for me. I give the word,

"I got something. 954 down on Simpson. Ten minutes."

So in ten minutes you're in the hallways down at 954 and you have your boys with you: What d'ya want, man? What do you want? And you? How many bags?

The cops watch the addicts. When they see them start walking, they know something's happening. They get a lot of pushers like that—by following the addicts. A pusher is never safe—never! I don't care how big or tough he is, there's always guys that will take him off—rob him of his stuff.

Sometimes I would take my stuff, and early in the morning I would put it around in different hiding places: one bag in this hallway, two bags on some rooftop, four in a garbage can, one in a pack of cigarettes by a stoop. And I'd have all these places marked with chalk—like a "J" and then a "1" or a "4." I knew where every marking was.

When a guy would come to me and say, "Gimme a bag," I'd tell him:

"Gimme your money. Over there in a pack of cigarettes."

Then a guy would say, "Gimme two bags."

"Over there in 857, behind the radiator."

Once in a while a couple of guys come back and say,

"Man! There's nothing there!"

A junkie will always try to outsmart you. He'll pull that kind of business any time he can get away with it.

"Man! You come in here askin' for a break—a half a dollar. I can't, Baby. I'm short."

"But I gotta go meet the man, and I ain't got my money. You know I gotta come in right, 'cause the last time I came in short. He told me, 'No, Baby, I can't do it. Sorry. Steal. Beg a half dollar on the corner. Do something.' "

One of those deals. They're hard, hard. Junkie pushers will do anything. And when they're down and out, you see them coming short. And then they end up taking you off, getting you hurt, or killed. You got to prove tougher than them, ready to go all the way. Rat race.

Then there's the "switch." A junkie knows that every pusher has his own special way of putting his stuff together: he packs his bags a certain way; he puts a little piece of tape over the fold; he wraps tape around the whole thing; all kinds of clues.

I had one guy who knew just the way I packed mine, and he pulled this "switch" deal on me.

"Two bags." He give me the money and walks away. I count the bills.

"Hey! Two dollars short, man!"

"Man, that's all I got. Gimme a break, Baby. I'm up tight, man. I'll come in later with it."

"Gimme the two dollars or gimme the two bags!"

"Please, man!"

"Listen! Gimme the money, hear?"

"All right, man. Here's your stuff," and he hands me the two bags.

"Here. Keep one bag."

"No man. That ain't no good. I need two bags for a fix; I can't make it with one."

So I take the bags, and give him back his money.

But what he gave me is not what I give him. They're two "lemons." He knows how I put my bags together, and he makes up these two empty bags just exactly the same as mine, so they look alike. Then he walks off with two bags of junk and the money, and I got two empty bags—two lemons in my pocket!

Of course, then what happens when you sell those bags to the next guy? He'll come back,

"What did you sell me those lemons for?"

"Are you kidding, man? I didn't sell you no lemon."

But the junkie will be fighting mad. Some guys have really gotten hurt like this. The junkie will go back and really get the pusher — even kill him. It's not always empty bags though, many times it's just "garbage"—a mixture made up just to cheat the next guy. Like baking powder, talcum, crushed aspirins, instead of heroin. Many times you cook it up and you can't even draw it up in the needle it's so thick. Some guys will stuff one empty bag inside another. You can't hardly see through them, so you can't tell unless you examine it real close. And when you're copping on the street, you don't stop to do that. You cop and go! Especially if you're dealing with a guy who's been selling dope for a long time.

Bags I sold in movie houses too—I'd give the word around the block that I was in this movie. Doorman knew who I was. I'd give him a cut. Guys would come in,

"Is Johnny here?"

"Down in the third row."

They would come down and sit next to me, and I'd pass the junk to them and they'd leave.

And public rest rooms I'd use. I'd get in one of those places and nod for hours. Guys knew I was going to be there and they'd come. TAP-TAP!

Or I'd go to a telephone booth and call a guy.

"OK, I'll meet you there," he says.

I put the bag in the change return place, and when I see him come by, I hang up and get out of the booth.

"Psst. Gimme the money. It's in the exchange."

Sometimes I would carry the bags in slits in my clothes. Or I would take rubber from balloons, wrap a bag of stuff in the rubber, and carry it in my mouth.

Some pushers have walkie-talkies. I remember up on Kelly Street, a guy was sitting there on the stoop with kids and everybody all around him, and he's got a walkie-talkie in his hand. All of a sudden it blasts on, "Yeah, I'm alone. The man wants two. You dig anything happening? Everything all right? OK, Al. Bring me two."

And a guy goes up through the hallways, up the stairs, bringing two bags of stuff. There's another guy on the roof watching everything. They're usually young guys—kids. No more than three in a setup like this; more than that and it gets out of order. Funny business.

Once in a while you find a "rat" pusher that has a grocery store or a candy store. He's just a natural hustler—do anything to turn a dollar. So he puts junk in his stock too. I know a guy, when you go in to buy groceries, you say to him, "Gimme two bombs," and he'll throw two decoxsin bottles (bombitas) right in on top of the bread and beans. Or "Gimme a couple spikes," and he reaches under the counter and comes up with two new needles. When you got a habit you know where to go. Ain't nothing as important as making a connection when you're hooked.

10. The Junkie

We were right in front of the door of death—murdering ourselves with drugs. We never knew if the next shot would be our last one. No human being could come far enough into our darkness to save us. We no longer considered ourselves human beings. We were hopeless dope fiends—animals. And there was nothing we could do about it, so we might as well go to sleep. There was no other way.

That was the only answer to every problem: Run for the needle! If you got in an argument, if you was alone, or scared, or bored, or sick, the answer was the same. You got no will power of your own. It's a terrible, terrible hard life, and you always lose.

Sometimes you wanted to explain yourself to someone, but nobody could help you. You felt nobody had the answer. There was no way out.

We used to walk around the block, around and around, getting dizzy. One day one of the guys took his hat and threw it on the floor and jumped on it,

"You don't know nobody! I don't know nobody! All we do is shoot drugs!"

We were high, you know, telling each other, "You're a bum!" So disgusted from dope, from stealing, from hurting our families, from people saying,

"Look at him, he's a dope fiend!"

You get busted and you go to jail, and when you come out you go back to the same neighborhood. The doors are still shut. No wonder they are; you're still an addict.

When you stop using drugs, you lose your best friends. You come around the block; nobody hardly talks to you. One of the guys says,

"Hi, how ya doing? I hear ya stopped, huh? That's good, man. Cool! Stay that way, man. So long. See ya. We're gonna shoot some drugs. . . . "

And you're walking alone. Things like that happen. So you think,

"Man! I'll go along and shoot with them."

But that's a drag, too. You still feel miserable. It's a plot and a half. You're lost without the drugs; you're lost with the drugs. It's driving you to commit suicide. You don't want to die; but you don't want to live either. It was like, "Well, if I live, I live; if I die, I die." You don't put no value on life. There's all sorts of confusion in your mind. There's no way out.

* * *

Sometimes the urge to see my children was so strong I went out and stood across the street from their school so I could see them as they came out. I had a burning desire to talk with them, to be able to hold them, and love them, and kiss them. But I couldn't. I was an outcast.

I remember one day standing on the corner. I was dirty. I had a beard, and my hair was long. I was a filthy mess, and I was high. I was just standing there "goofing" as we call it, when there was a tug at my sleeve. I turned with a quickening in my heart as I recognized my daughter—my oldest girl, Laurie. I reached out to touch her and she backed away, "Don't, Daddy." Tears streamed down her pretty cheeks and I wanted to hold her and wipe them away. "Daddy," she said again, sobbing, "please go away."

"What?" I squeezed out in torment. I wanted to say more. I wanted to tell her how sorry I was for all the shame she felt. I wanted to promise her that tomorrow, next week, next year, I would have a job and we would all be happy and together again. But I couldn't say another word. My lips and my life were bound. Up tight. And I knew it would never be more than a passing wish.

"My friends are looking at you, Daddy. Please, please go away!" I fumbled for a cigarette as she turned and ran across the street where her friends stood whispering and staring at me, "Laurie's father's a no-good junkie." I knew what they were saying; and I turned into the crowd with the tears running over my face, and the words numbing my brain: "Laurie's daddy's a junkie." It was true. A wasted, no-good junkie.

But junkies keep trying. Everything there is—hospitals, jails, people, counselors, psychiatrists, psychologists, running away to Puerto Rico, doing this, doing that, trying to smoke marijuana again so we can get our mind off dope, trying to drink, getting pills. There comes a time when we use everything at once. Pleasures — women, wine, song, dope. Nothing ever helps.

So frustrated we want to die. Then we start thinking how stupid we were to first inject that needle in our arm—thinking it was only a kick. And it turned out to be a nightmare. And there was no way back.

Life becomes a big dark hole for an addict. We get so frustrated—that we actually want to die, to end everything.

"Death might just be the very best high of all," one of the guys said one time. It's easy to think that when it looks like there's no way out. Death—completely relaxed. Not a problem in the world! Yeah, man! That's outta sight—no feeling at all.

Part 2:

THE ADDICTS

11. The Road To Damascus

> "I believe in nothing but myself and my experiences. The world consists of me, myself and my feelings. Everything else is mere fancy."

I used to quote that all the time—knew the whole thing. It's me! I create the dreams. I create the world today and tomorrow. When I cease to be, everything ceases to be. That's how I talked.

When I was a child my father and mother dedicated me to God's work. I didn't know this until recently, but they did. And Mother used to have dreams about me standing behind a pulpit. I didn't want any part of that business. I used to make fun of her and say, "God and me—we can't make it together."

I'd become a pretty nasty atheist; talked against God every chance I got. But I had a desire and a curiosity about Him. There was a battle going on inside me. Everytime I would hear something about God, I'd try to get away from it. I remember many times in the prison I used to put on the earphones on Sunday and listen to the radio. I would never go to church, but I'd listen to a broadcast; and if there'd be a story about Christ, all of a sudden something would happen to me. I'd feel this heat building up in me, and tears coming into my eyes. One time the man on the radio was talking about Pontius Pilate at the trial of Jesus Christ. When he said Pilate decided to wash his hands of Christ, I saw the whole thing. I had to take off the earphones. The tears built up. And when I read *The Robe* I could only read just so much at a time, and something so big would stir inside of me that I couldn't stand it.

Then one day in jail, Roy, one of the prisoners, started telling me about a place where dope addicts were getting "delivered." He said it was a church called "Damasco." That let me out; I didn't want to hear about any church. I used to be hard on him — called him all kinds of names.

"You creep! Get outa here. I don't wanna listen."

"I don't care what you wanna do, Gimenez. When I get outa here I'm gonna go there myself and see what's happening."

I used to call him "the Billy Graham of the Bronx County Jail": "Here comes Billy! Here's that Bible-preachin' prisoner!" But the funny thing was when he talked I did listen. I was 30 years old and I wanted to change.

The same day I got out of Bronx County Jail it happened like always. I took a shot of dope. Then I went home, and when my mother saw me she started to cry. She was so upset she told me to leave. I went out and took a 7th Avenue Express train. I fell asleep as I was riding, and passed my station by two stops. I started to walk back—when you get high you like to walk; and I took a little shortcut through the park. As I was passing 162nd Street I saw this sign that said "Damasco" and a brightly lit cross stood out against the dark sky. I remembered this was the same name that Roy had mentioned in prison. Since I was high I decided to check it out.

When I walked inside and upstairs I saw they were having a service. There were guys I had seen in the streets, guys that were shooting dope with me. Something was strange though; some of them looked high—their eyes were shining, but they were praying. And I thought to myself, "What's with these guys? What kind of game they got going here?"

A man up in front was talking about a camp. He said they couldn't send nobody else to camp because they didn't have no more money. I had a few dollars and there's some nice looking girls across the way. When the offering plate came by I figured I'd put in a dollar bill to make me look good to them. I went into my pocket and pulled out a bill and dropped it in the plate. Then as the plate moved down the row I saw I'd put in a five dollar bill! And I couldn't reach to grab it! I knew I wasn't going to leave that place until I got my money back. I was all full of tension during the service, trying to figure it out: What will I tell this guy? And I wondered if this whole thing was a fix. I wasn't hooked, just coming out of jail; yet my mind was hooked, and I needed that money for dope.

After the service I went up to the pastor and said,

"Listen, Reverend, I'm a junkie and I just got out of jail." I was trying to put the scare in this guy. He was a little guy, about five foot two, skinny, big eyebrows, but he looked right through me into my soul, and he said,

"I'm sorry. We have no more room."

"Look, I didn't come lookin' for charity. My own family won't give it to me; I don't expect strangers to."

That did something to him, and he said gently,

"Would you sit down a minute?"

"But look . . . "

"We'll find a place for you."

"But I don't want to stay here. I just got out of jail."

"Then you *should* stay here 'cause if you don't you're going to go right back. I know you've already taken that first shot, right?"

All of a sudden I felt I gotta get away from this man. I became afraid of him and I never did get to ask him about my money.

He went on. "You must stay here with us tonight."

And I began to think up excuses, "No, I hafta go someplace. Some people are expecting me."

"Where are they?"

"Oh, just some friends of mine."

"Are you coming back?"

"Yeah." I didn't have no intention of coming back if I could get away.

"When?" He kept pushing me.

"Oh, I'll be back tonight."

"What time?" He pinned me down.

"11:30." I grabbed a figure out of the air. "Yeah! I'll be back at 11:30."

"All right. Be here at 11:30." He looked right into my eyes. "I'll be waiting for you."

I got up out of there and ran back to my own neighborhood. Right away I found a girl, and we got a shot of dope and a room where we could stay. But we decided to go out and get a hot dog first. She was talking about all her tricks, and we were sitting there eating when all of a sudden I looked at the clock and it was twenty minutes after eleven. I hadn't even finished my hot dog, but I got up to leave.

"Where ya going, Johnny?" She looked surprised.

"I'll see ya."

"But where ya going?"

"Never mind. See ya 'round," and I ran out the door and kept going for fifteen blocks. I remember it was 11:30 when I got to the front door of the Damascus Church. The Reverend, Pop Rosado, was standing right there. He didn't say a word; he just pointed. One of the boys took me upstairs and gave me a bed.

The next day all day long I was sneaking a drink from a bottle of whiskey. I'd walk to the corner, then I'd walk back. I wanted to leave, and I wanted to stay. Then they told me, "You're going to camp." And they made a special trip to Mountaindale, New York, just to take me. We stopped once to buy groceries and I got out of the car and started to walk away. But BOOM! I turned around and came back and got right in the car again.

When we first got to the camp I saw all these guys jumping around and praising God out loud. This was way out. A couple of them were embracing each other. I thought this was funny business; I couldn't see it—two men embracing. Right away my mind went to the wrong, the bad. A guy came over to welcome me; it was someone I'd committed a burglary with. He comes up with,

"Johnny! Man, I'm happy to see you. You came to the right place."

I thought he was stone out of his mind; I thought he'd gone crazy.

"What's wrong with you?"

"Man! What's wrong with me? Listen! I got Jesus."

"OK. Take it easy. What's going on here, really?"

He cooled down a little, and grinned at me,

"Something's gonna happen to you." And he went on to tell me about God, and about this Mountaindale Camp, and about what had already happened to some of the junkies I knew, and how it was all part of that little Spanish church — Damasco — where Pop Rosado took me in when even my own family had locked me out.

A little while later the guys had me on my knees and they were praying and they had their hands on me,

"Lord, save him. Lord, heal him."

I got mad. I didn't go for all this business. So I stayed way back in the back of the church. The leader of the guys — there was about eighteen of us—was Jackie Dean. We used to call him "The Chicken." That wasn't because he was chicken-hearted, but because he looked like a chicken. He was a knife man. I didn't know him, but I knew of him up in the Bronx. Up at Mountaindale he had something happen to him. He was still a leader though and he would talk to us,

"Aw, you think you're tough guys. You walk around here talkin' outa the side of your mouth. You're shadow boxing; you're not tough. You're nothing but a bunch of juvenile delinquents. You should have your diapers on, cause you're not men. Let me tell you. Man! you don't know nothing."

I thought he was talking right to me all the time, and I was thirty years old! He got me so mad; everything he'd say would be me. And I'd get tempted.

"One of these days," I'd say, "I'm gonna punch him so hard in the mouth he's not gonna know whether he's comin' or goin'."

"You been a phony all your life," he'd say. "You live on dreams and make believe."

Oh! I was really out to get this guy. But one day I was sitting in the back of the church with Pee Wee. I knew him from the Bronx. If a dope pusher wouldn't give Pee Wee the dope he wanted, he'd stab him. That's how he happened to turn up at Damasco—he was hiding from the police 'cause he thought he'd killed a man. Now up here in the camp Pee Wee was telling me.

"Johnny, I thought I had heart. But Man! I didn't know what heart was till I stopped bullying people and let God show me how to love them instead."

12. Pee Wee

Pee Wee grew up in Puerto Rico till he was about eight years old. Then his sister left for New York. She wrote back to the family telling how New York was so beautiful and so big! And she asked why her mother didn't come over too.

Pee Wee's family had a good grocery store business so when his mother said she'd like to go to New York, her husband was able to give her the money. He sent her and Pee Wee off to America by themselves. After they found an apartment they wrote him to come join them. Pee Wee's father sold his business in San Juan and came up to New York City.

He didn't have to work at first because he had enough money. He used to take Pee Wee to school every morning.

"We walked together, and he was very close to me," Pee Wee told me. "I liked to have him there. Some days we would see little girls and he would tell me how one day I would get married to a beautiful senorita."

Then one morning, while Pee Wee was still in bed, he heard his father say,

"Beding—(that was his pet name for his son) when he gets up, give him this half dollar and tell him to go to school. When I come back from the hospital, I will pick him up at school."

He went to the hospital and Pee Wee went to school. He was big; he weighed 225 pounds. He was healthy; he never went into the hospital before. But when Pee Wee came out of school that day, his father wasn't there. And when he went home, his father wasn't there.

"Where's Dad?" Pee Wee asked.

His mother said, "He'll be back. You know he went to the hospital."

They waited and waited. That night Pee Wee's sister went to the hospital and they told her they were going to keep him there, because he had something wrong in his stomach.

The next day Pee Wee went to the hospital, but they wouldn't let him go up to see his father because he was too young. So he used to go out on the sidewalk every afternoon and look up to his window.

One day they operated on him, and he died. Pee Wee was just ten. And from that time on he didn't go to school like he used to. He started missing; and he started fighting. Everytime he heard someone mention the name of his father, it would hurt him so much he would have to fight. He used to like to see people dancing, having a good time. Everything was different after his father died. He was a very humble man—never would argue with nobody. Pee Wee seen people try to pick a fight with him, but he wouldn't ever fight back.

After his father died all this came over him. He wanted to get even with people. He would fight for anything. He was the only one in the family who was violent. Before he was eleven, he was already drinking wine with the gang.

One day after he got on drugs, he and Tino went to get some dope from the Comanches gang. While they were there some fellows came in and called out,

"C'mon, need all you guys. We're gonna fight the Viceroys!"

They gave Pee Wee and Tino a shotgun and a .32 pistol, and they all went to this other neighborhood to get the Viceroys. During the fight one of the Viceroys got shot, and the cops picked up Pee Wee and his friend for it. Pee Wee was under age, 15, so they sent him away to Otisville Training School for a year and a half.

After he came out Pee Wee found a girl and was living with her, but she left him. He was going crazy without her — nearly lost his mind. That's when he started sticking up people to get dope. When he would sign into a hospital to "rest up" they'd have to give him five or six shots to keep him quiet. When he would be in his bed, he would be fighting — real nervous. People would just look at him and he'd snap at them.

"What're ya lookin' at me for?" And he'd want to fight.

Shortly before he came to Damascus there was this boy sleeping in the same basement with Pee Wee. He used to go around and steal and come back and give Pee Wee stuff. Then one day when he had some stuff, he wouldn't give Pee Wee any and they got in an argument.

While they was talking, Pee Wee seen a shadow and he turned around with his knife open and stabbed somebody. He didn't even look to see who it was; he just ran. But his friends later told him it was this boy's father and he was dying.

The next day Pee Wee went over to see Norman Eddy at East Harlem Protestant Parish. He said,

"Mr. Eddy, I need help." Pee Wee didn't tell him what he had done, but he asked, "Can you get me into a hospital? Man, I'm up tight."

"Pee Wee, how can I help you? You've been to all the hospitals. I've sent you every place I know. Where could you go?"

"Look. I gotta go somewhere."

"The only place you could go is Central Islip Hospital. And if you go there you'll have to sign yourself in for three years voluntarily."

Now Pee Wee was hooked; he had a big habit. But he wanted to kick 'cause he was scared the cops were onto him, so he told Mr. Eddy,

"Yeah! I'll do anything."

Mr. Eddy got him into the hospital, and he signed for three years. But after eight days, Pee Wee couldn't take it anymore, so he told the people,

"Look, I wanna sign out."

"You can't sign out. The minute you go out, the sheriff will grab you and put you in jail."

"But I can't stay here!"

So he signed out. And when he walked out, there was nobody there waiting for him. The next day he went to Manhattan early in the morning to see Norman Eddy again to tell him he couldn't stay in the hospital.

"Have you had any breakfast, Pee Wee?" He was very rundown and skinny.

"No, I don't have any money."

Mr. Eddy gave him a little ticket which was good for breakfast at a nearby restaurant, and Pee Wee walked over and ate by himself. As he was coming out of the restaurant, he saw the man he had stabbed standing there looking at him. This was the first that Pee Wee knew the man wasn't dead. But he was scared and he darted across the street and got on a bus. He was sure the man had gone to call the cops. Pee Wee was nervous as he rode along, and he was fidgeting with a slip of paper in his pocket. He unfolded it and read it, remembering that Norman Eddy had given it to him the day he went to the hospital.

"Pee Wee, if you can't make it in the hospital, try this church. This is the only other place I know."

It was the address of the Damascus Christian Church, and as Pee Wee got off in the Bronx, he was heading for the church. He didn't go with any idea in his head except that he didn't want to get caught by the police. He had to have some place to stay, and he knew he couldn't go back, or somebody'd call the cops on him.

He hadn't been at the church very long when his sister came in bringing him fruit punches. She found out where he was from Norman Eddy and she came in and out of the church for several days, just keeping an eye on her brother. She was watching the other boys too; and one day she decided she wanted God to come into her life, and change her like He had changed the addicts she met there. Then Pee Wee saw the change in his sister's life, and he went off by himself to a little room and just started talking to God.

"Look, if You're real — they tell me You are real. I don't know nothing. I don't even know how to read the Bible. I don't know how to read — nothin'! I lost my family; I ain't nobody."

And he was just talking and crying. And he kept on crying like he couldn't stop. And it was like some big hand was just squeezing his heart — there was a pain, but it was with a joy. And he seemed to know that he wouldn't be the same anymore. Everything would be different. And no matter what happened, he would be safe.

13. Something New Inside

That night in the church there at Mountaindale—while I was sitting with Pee Wee—something happened to me. I looked at Pee Wee; then I looked at myself. Like I never had before. It was like I come out of myself and I stood there watching. I could see everything from afar; my own life was going on before me. I sort of saw myself sitting down, like a lonely little kid, watching a bunch of other kids playing—having a good time. But not me; I wasn't having a good time.

Then all of a sudden I seemed to say to myself, "Well, why don't you go and play too? Why don't you go and have a good time? Why are you sitting off here all by yourself? You can have a good time too."

That night I went to bed, but I woke up about three o'clock in the morning. Jackie Dean was shouting,

"Devil, get outa here. Leave this place right now. In the name of Jesus, go."

I opened my eyes and I could see like he was fighting someone.

"You have no power in here. We rebuke you in the name of Jesus."

All of a sudden I became afraid. I could see the tension in Jackie Dean's face, and this tremendous fear came over me — like all the demons of hell were loose in the room at that moment. Something tremendous was going on, but I didn't know what, and I was almost crying. The guys were waking up and getting down on their knees to pray. Here were guys who had done time in prison, guys who had hurt people, and they were scared. I seen guys stabbed; I been shot at; I fought in gangs. But nothing ever bothered me like this. I really became afraid—for the first time. I called out, "Lord, help me. Protect me." I was afraid—like a little baby, lost in the night.

We all went outside and stood on the porch. It was a beautiful night in April. The stars were out so bright and we stood there looking up at the sky. One by one the boys went back in, but something held me there. I'd been there a few minutes when this boy, Georgie, came to me and said,

"Why don't you come inside, Johnny?"

I felt something was going to happen, like someone was waiting for me.

"You go in," I told him. "I'll be in in a little while."

I walked off to the side of the building, but I kept looking around as though I expected someone to show up at any minute. I wanted to kneel, 'cause I knew I had to talk to God, but I made sure nobody was around first. I remember looking up at the night sky—I've always loved the sky. But this time I saw the stars—really saw the sparkle and shine, and I could almost see the hand of God in the heavens placing them in their orbits. They wasn't just little pinpricks; they became big and real and full of personality. I felt so much the beauty of God in the heavens that I grabbed hold of the railing and knelt there with tears rolling down from my eyes. And I began to cry,

"God. God. God. Please help me!"

I didn't know what to say; I just knew that something had to come out of me. And as I cried, all my past seemed to come in front of me. I saw so many horrible things I done. I saw my mother crying. I hurt so many people, caused so much pain, brought so much shame on my parents, my wife, my kids. I began sobbing,

"Please, please, God. Help me! I'm sick and I'm rotten through and through. I'm no good, God! Please help me!"

I was banging my chest up against the banister like I was trying to destroy myself. And I kept crying and crying, weeping way down deep inside. Then all of a sudden I felt something warm come over me. I felt like God had just opened up the skies, and had come down to take hold of me. All I could think of was that God had me in His hand, and He was shaking me—like when someone takes dirty clothes and puts them in the washer, and it has to bang away and shake them. That was what was happening to me. God was putting me in the washer and He was washing me clean.

Somewhere in the background I could hear voices like from afar, "Jesus hear him. Praise the Lord." Then Jackie Dean told everybody to go inside; and after everyone had left, I opened my eyes and everything was still. Nothing was moving, not even wind at that moment—like the whole world had just stopped. I got up and I remembered I felt light; all the heaviness had gotten out of me, and I felt like something new was inside. I just stood still in the quiet, and I felt the tears. And from deep inside of me the name of Jesus kept rolling, not from my mouth, but from way down deep, "Jesus, Jesus, Jesus."

I started walking down the road and I looked up and saw big clouds over me. I began half-walking, half-running, and the clouds stayed over me; and I expected God to descend out of that cloud and pick me up and put me up there in the sky with Him. I really expected Him. I was weeping and laughing—I felt good; it was such joy. I was jumping down the road like a little kid in the dark of night. Like it was my birthday, and I knew there would be a lot of gifts waiting for me when I got home. But it wasn't dark; the road seemed very light, like a light was shining. I walked for miles and I was singing,

"Jesus, Jesus. Praise your name! Thank you, Lord. Come here, Jesus."

I expected God to come down and put His arm around me. I didn't realize He was inside me all that time. I walked and walked and walked. Oh, such a joyful time! It was seven o'clock when I got back to the camp, and I was so tired I walked in and just dropped on my bed. The boys didn't bother me when they got up. Somebody put a blanket over me and I slept all morning. When I got up around noon to eat lunch, I couldn't stop crying. Somebody said, "Let's pray," and I jumped up and said,

"Oh, Jesus, Jesus, Jesus."

Everytime anybody would say the name of Jesus it was like an electric shock to me. I couldn't help it. The battle inside me was being won, and Jesus was the winner.

God brings His Holy Spirit into messed up humans, and that bursting forth of Him in us is so peaceful and beautiful and sweet. We struggled so hard for so long to keep our bodies satisfied, and suddenly here was this wonderful Holy Spirit satisfying both our flesh and our spirit.

It's like coming home—you can kick off your shoes, and there's a fire burning and a cup of hot tea steaming beside you, and a soothing wife to be there close. This is the kind of thing that happens when I read the Bible. I feel at peace, at ease. The one who has been kicked out by his family, the one who has no place to call his own — he can come home in the Word of God. Here is the addict's new home! It's a beautiful thing — a free thing!

When I found Jesus, man! it was like an explosion! All of a sudden everything happened. You see, in Mountaindale there is no patrol, nothing to hold you down. The guys meet Jesus and all of a sudden—BOOM! we find a love like we never had before, and we just about go crazy in that love!

I was up there at the camp about eight months all told. It was so beautiful. I was reading the Bible and the Scripture I loved so much was,

"I am persuaded that neither death, nor life, nor angels, nor principalities, nor powers, nor things present, nor things to come, nor height, nor depth, nor any other creature, shall be able to separate us from the love of God, which is in Christ Jesus our Lord."

I used to read this and it would roll around inside of me. And sometimes I'd be sitting down praying and I could see Gethsemane and Jesus. I could see when He wept and when He walked with His disciples—everything came so alive to me. Like I was seeing a movie right in front of me. It was so great!

Part of the newness came out of me wanting to do things—right away I began to work! I'd been on the go all my life, but I never liked to work. I'd be hustling here and pushing there, making connections, doing a lot of low rotten things, beating people up. It took a lot of energy; it was work of a kind. But I'd never *worked* really—not with my hands before.

Now I wanted to do something for God. I wanted to build; I wanted to see things grow. I began to put in plumbing; I began to cook in the kitchen. I was enjoying working for the first time in my life, and I was thirty years old.

14. Damasco

Some addicts found new life in Christ right there at Damascus Christian Church. Others of us had to spend a lot of time at Mountaindale. We needed time to get far away from the streets of the Bronx before we could get free. But all of us—directly or indirectly—trace our "delivery" to that little Spanish church at 861 East 162nd Street. It was God's house all right. He was there. You go inside Damasco, and boy! something happens to you! It's like the excitement and the gripping power of a new love affair.

You see the cracks all over the walls, and you see a young man coming downstairs mopping the floor, and another one sweeping. "Glory! Hallelujah!" sings through the halls; and downstairs you hear somebody holler,

"Chow! Come and get it or we'll throw it away!"

You see a bunch of boys running down the stairs from a room that has no door, just a curtain over the front. When you pull back the curtain you see a row of beds. Over in the corner a guy is trembling. Over by the window another guy is standing with a Bible in his hand. Then you hear somebody call out, "In the Name of Jesus Christ, be healed!"

In the office one woman is typing and another is calling people on the phone. In the little parlor you see Mom Rosado sitting with the Bible in her lap and she's got two or three boys sitting around, listening to her explain the message of God. In the temple a couple boys are kneeling together in front of the cross.

It isn't a beautiful place by normal standards; yet it's the loveliest place in the world because it's God's factory. It belongs to my Father.

And people come in — broken people, rotten people, no goods, unwanteds. The misfits of society walk through those open doors to new life. This church belongs to them, and right away when they come they're in the presence of God. When I first walked in Damasco I thought to myself, "These guys are all high!" They were high all right; they were flying. Pop Rosado didn't only preach to the misfits who wandered in off the street; he practiced. He loved a soul beyond his own life; in fact, he was ministering to a boy when he caught a heart attack and died a few months later. But he taught a lot of us guys what it means to love people. And Mom kept right on after he passed away. She'd do anything to help a junkie get straight and stay clean.

Damasco was like the center of new life for addicts; and out from the temple there stretched life lines into the gutters of the great city of New York, and then further out into the towns and cities across America.

15. The Birth of "The Addicts"

I believe that God needs each and every one of us. We become a vital part in the mechanism of salvation. You see, this is the thing—to be needed. In a very real sense, God coming into a person's life makes that person feel needed by God. And God, in filling a person with His Holy Spirit is admitting that He needs men, that He needs human beings to contain His Spirit. This realization raises a person immediately in his own eyes. Man! You become valuable. It makes you feel important. That's as it should be; you should feel important in God's plan.

It came to me that everyone is looking for recognition; and when you come at last to God, you become a child of the King. You're a prince! And it doesn't matter what condition you're in, or how good you are, He makes you a prince!

This is what does it—this is what gives you the sense of belonging, of being "in": the Holy Spirit comes to dwell in you, and you all of a sudden know that God cares so much about you. He'd have to, to send His Spirit into you, to motivate you, to control you, to lead you, and to fill you with so much.

I went into a bar in Chicago one day to see a guy. I knew him; he was an alcoholic. His wife asked me to go in and help him. I like him; he's a real serious guy. When I saw him sitting there I felt this man was seeking recognition in a glass of beer. Somehow or other he was getting a personality out of this glass of beer. He was somebody at that moment. And yet when he saw me, like a blankness came into him. He bowed his head and said to me,

"I'm sorry you walked in here. I feel bad enough."

And I thought, "God, what can I tell him?" And the first thing that came to me in the Spirit was this, "We need your help."

He looked at me; he didn't expect this. I told him,

"You know, we're starting a work here; and I feel you can be such a tremendous help to Rudy—you know, Rudy's a young man. And there are so many people around here you could understand and help—alcoholics and addicts."

He sensed something. I don't understand it completely, but I feel God did something. God gave him to see that he could be an important personality. He could be a prince. This is the most important thing—to be needed.

About two months after I was converted, the Lord gave me a vision of being useful to Him.

Some of the guys had gathered to pray in an old hut on the property at Mountaindale when God spoke to me. It was about two o'clock in the morning, and we had all joined hands in prayer. God used Don—he spoke like a Hebrew, beautiful! And then God gave me the interpretation:

"I will give you the material, and you shall build my tabernacle. I will send you throughout the world, and the world shall behold my glory."

This thought has come back to me time and time again—in different ways: "Ye shall be as doves and I will make you to fly throughout the world, and they shall behold my glory." Always in this prophecy there has been the figure eight, and I always wondered, "Why eight?" Then I discovered that eight means "new beginning"; and the number became very significant. From that moment on I began to pray for eight boys to make up the "material" for His "tabernacle."

While I was back in the city at Damasco I met Louis. He was doing a lot of painting with oil colors, and I took him with me to Rockaway. We would sleep in the back of this church there, and we'd go around together and testify. And the idea started to form in my mind about a play we could put on—showing the way we used to be before God took over our lives, and how there is a way out.

The first time we got to do anything was at a church out on Far Rockaway, where the pastor was an ex-gang fighter. Louis and I got six other guys to join us: Frankie and Lennie came along, and Ronnie and Wayne, and there was Leon and Sambo too. We planned out how we could go through all the motions we had gone through so long, and it would let people know some of the horrors of drug addiction. We laid it out in six acts: One, "The Gallery"—where the addicts congregate to take off; Two, "Rude Awakening"—the terrible truth seeps into the mind of the parent—his son is a dope addict; Three, "The Kid"—a year later, he's lost in the abyss of addiction; Four, "Cold Turkey"—the horrible terrors of withdrawal; Five, "Overdose"—the final curtain when there's no way out; Six, "Conversion"—there is an answer.

That night on Far Rockaway, the drama was rough, but it seemed to pack a wallop, and we decided to try it again back in the Bronx. We all knew it could help lots of guys on the street.

The first thing we wanted to do with the play was to warn young kids of the awfulness of dope addiction. Then we wanted to let addicts know they aren't hopelessly twisted forever. We wanted to tell them that Jesus can fill up the empty spaces in their lives and completely change their way of living. We wanted to tell everybody what Jesus Christ has done for us—how He broke the chains that bound us to heroin, and made us free.

People who saw the play were pretty shook up, but they wanted their friends to see it too. We got asked to do it for a youth rally at Hunt's Point Palace in the Bronx; and about 200 more people saw it there. From that point doors started swinging open to many churches, and we went down to McKeesport, Pennsylvania, where Reverend Beatrice LaMonte was pastor.

Down there the Lord spoke to me about taking this play out all over America. God used this woman there to really teach us to live on faith. She was a very compassionate minister, and God used her as a kind of spark plug for us.

"Step out, Johnny," she told me. "Don't worry. Let God take care of you. He wants to."

We got invited to give the play in churches all around the McKeesport area. We asked "Aunt Bea" if she would kind of act as our secretary and take care of the letters that had to be written, booking us into more and more churches. While we were there we got together $200 and made a payment on a brand new truck so we could get around the country. Frankie had learned to sew while he was in prison, and he made us curtains we could use wherever we went to put on the drama. That was when we began getting invited to go to jails and some schools, and everywhere we went we had a chance to tell how Jesus Christ was the great Healer, the great Deliverer — not only from dope but from anything that got us up tight.

From Erie, Pennsylvania, we got invited to Illinois. There we met some people who introduced us to a Christian businessman in Denver, and we made the big jump out to the beautiful Rocky Mountain country. The whole idea was really growing, and God was bringing us guys along too. One night He gave me special words we could sing to the old "Battle Hymn of the Republic" as part of the drama. I was sleeping, and all of a sudden I heard that music, and the words were like marching right in front of me. I grabbed a paper and pencil and wrote them down. No effort at all. I wrote songs before, but I used to break my head to get the words right. Man! Sit down and figure out the rhymes; it was work. But here it was three o'clock in the morning, and the words were just going by me in writing! Right away I started waking up people, trying to sing it to them. That was something!

After Denver, we went back to the Bronx and had a reshuffle. Sambo left to study at the Bible Institute in Zion, Rhode Island; Lennie felt called to be an evangelist; Ronnie was asked to be a counselor at a camp for kids who were growing up the same way we did; and Leon stayed in the city. That cut the group in half; but Juggy, Rudy, Jerry and Julio were all ready to go on the road, so the new "eight" left New York City for Chicago to present "The Addicts" real life drama, at the Conrad Hilton Hotel for an annual Christian businessmen's convention.

16. Snuffy

While we were at the convention, Snuffy was out walking the streets of Chicago. He'd been down on Madison Street shooting dope and drinking wine and jack-rolling people. He and this pickpocket were working together, and they was on the corner drinking and robbing people, when Snuffy looked at him and said,

"Man! Why don't we go up to the Loop and get some money? These people ain't got no money down here."

The pickpocket agreed; so the two of them walked together and on the way they decided they would steal a car—they could get $400 easy that way! He jumped in this car, trying to wire it up; but Snuffy could see the guy wasn't getting no place 'cause he was too drunk. So he asked the pickpocket,

"Why don't you just give me my money? And I'll go my way, and you go your way."

They chopped their money up—the pickpocket got his end and Snuffy got his end, and they separated. Snuffy kept on walking up the street taking things out of cars. And all the time these two detectives was watching him, and they finally snatched him on Michigan Avenue, about 3:30 in the morning, just a block from the Conrad Hilton Hotel. They put him up against the wall and said,

"You get up here, Tramp. What are you doing up here anyway? Bumming these people, getting in these cars, stealing things?"

"Man, I ain't been doin' that!"

They shook him down and found two pints of wine, and they throwed them in the alley, and they took all Snuffy's money and told him,

"Now you get back down on Madison Street where you belong."

"OK, Man. Don't lock me up; I'll go."

Sure enough, they let him go, and he started walking down the alley. Then he began thinking, "Man! 3:30 in the morning. I got to have me a drink, Man! I can't wake up in the morning this way."

Snuffy went back to the Avenue and peeked around the corner to see if the detectives was gone. He looked around real good, and saw three men standing in front of the hotel. Right away he thought, "There's me three suckers over there." So he walked over to them and he bummed them,

"Hey, brother, how about helpin' an old Georgia boy out on the road? He's about starvin' to death—ain't eat in about three or four days. If he had a dollar he could get him a 52¢ flop and a bowl of soup."

One of the men looked down at Snuffy and said,

"Brother, what's your name?"

"My name's J. R. Helton. My old man owns that hotel there, but I can't get no money off him this time of night."

Snuffy could get a conversation started like that with anybody. I never seen him to fail.

One of the men put his hand on Snuffy's shoulder and asked,

"J.R., can I pray for you?"

Snuffy looked at him like he was crazy—pray for a junkie? Knock him in the head for a quarter? But something let it out that night and without thinking Snuffy said,

"Yeah. I need a lot of it."

One man took his right arm and one took his left arm, and one put his hand on Snuffy's neck, and they marched him right on into the hotel lobby and set him down in a chair.

One of the men said, "OK, now J. R., we gonna pray for you. You wanna pray along with us?"

"Man, I don't know no prayin'. Let me outa here!"

"That's all right. Just put your head down. We're gonna pray anyhow."

And they did. They started praying and they was praying in more tongues than you ever heard. Snuffy thought they was crazy—like they just got out of a psycho ward. They prayed for him this way for about fifteen minutes. Nobody else was in the lobby at all until this preacher come by and said he couldn't sleep.

He asked, "Can I help you pray for this boy?"

And Snuffy jumped up and held them all back, "Wait just a

minute, fellas. These people ain't gonna pray for me. It ain't gonna do no good.'

But the preacher looked him in the eye and said,

"Everybody needs prayer."

They all four started praying for him now, and when they got through the preacher asked Snuffy,

"How do you feel now?"

"Well, I feel a little better, Preacher, but I gotta problem."

"What is it?"

"I ain't got no place to stay."

"Don't worry, you have now." And he put his arm around Snuffy and took him in the elevator four stories up to his room. When he unlocked the door and took Snuffy inside, he turned to him and said,

"J.R., God told me to go downstairs. 'Somebody downstairs needs some help,' and He led me right to you. I'm going to let you have this room now, and I'm going to get another one. It looks like you need a room. Will you stay here till in the morning?"

Snuffy looked at him like he was crazy, "Who me? Stay here till morning?" He needed a drink. He looked around and seen all the suits and all the clothes and he told the man,

"Sure, Preacher, I'll stay here."

"Now, I'm going to pray for you all night. God's got something good for you. I don't know what it is, but I'll be back here in the morning. You be here."

"OK, Preacher, I will."

He went out and shut the door and Snuffy laid back across the bed, and looked around at everything in the room and he thought, "This man is some kind of a nut. He's crazy—some kind of Billy Graham. Take me off the street, and put me up here with all these suitcases and all these clothes? Man, I think I'm gonna get up here and get everything he's got and make it. Get me some dope and some wine."

But something said, "No, it's too late. Why don't you just stay here till in the morning? You can get up and shave, and then get everything, and leave before he gets here."

So that's what he did. After he slept awhile in a clean bed, he got up and shaved and took a bath, and put on one of the preacher's sport coats and a pair of his pants. Then he grabbed one of his suitcases and took his big Texan hat—he just bought a new one and it was on the dresser. He set everything down at the door just as the key turned on the other side, and the door pushed open. The preacher come in on him just that fast.

"OK, hold it now, Preacher! Don't you call no police. Just give me my old dirty clothes and I'll go back on Madison Street, and we'll forget the whole thing."

"J.R., don't you worry. We're not going to call the police. You know something? You can lie to man. You can lie to anybody. But you can't lie to God. Come on, let's sit down and talk.

And he got on the phone and asked three or four more preachers to come up to his room. They all started preaching to Snuffy, and all the time something was going on in Snuffy's heart. When the others left, the preacher had some breakfast sent up and they stayed together all day. Finally he asked Snuffy,

"J.R., will you go somewhere tonight with me?"

"Preacher, I'll go anywhere you want to."

They went down through the lobby to the ballroom. It was the Christian businessmen's convention going on, and Snuffy was sitting at the table with all these preachers, and they was praying for him. During the preaching, Snuffy put his head down on the table and said,

"God, if You can do anything with an old con man and a junkie, go ahead and do it, and I'll serve You the rest of my days. I ain't no good; I know that. I been a thief all my life, a junkie for eleven years," and tears started coming down his cheek. The preacher noticed and said,

"J.R., accept the Lord right now."

And Snuffy told him, "I have."

"Come on, then," he said. "Let's go up on the stage and give your testimony."

It seemed like something just picked him up out of his chair and got him up on the stage. Four thousand people was out there in front of him, and he started speaking,

"I been on every skid row in the world, and done everything in the book. But something's happened to me this night, and I don't know what it is."

Oral Roberts looked at him and said, "Brother, this has got to be true, and it's got to be God."

And Snuffy told him, "If it weren't true, I'd never be up here."

After he give his name, he went back and set down, and right away here come a woman and a man and they start hugging him. He didn't know them from Adam's apple! And the woman said,

"Snuffy, is it really true?"

And he looked at her and said, "Sure it's true."

"You know, your sister in Atlanta, Georgia, has been praying for you for fifteen years. I'm Mrs. McJenkins, and this is my husband. Your sister is one of our very best friends, and we've often heard her pray for you. I think we should go call her up and tell her what's happened tonight."

When they got a call through to Atlanta, Georgia, Snuffy talked to his sister for thirty minutes, and she started crying,

"Snuffy, if the Lord can save you, He can save anybody!"

Mr. McJenkins was interested in helping Snuffy find a job, so he called a lawyer friend over to talk with them. They thought they would send Snuffy to a farm to work, but Snuffy didn't think he could make it there, 'cause he'd probably sneak wine all the time out there.

It was just about that very minute that I came walking by where they was talking, and the lawyer reached out and grabbed me by the arm,

"Johnny, you were a junkie, right? I want you to meet somebody here. This is Snuffy, J. R. Helton. He was a junkie for eleven years. I want you to take him with you on the road, Johnny. If he needs anything you get in touch with me; I'll stand behind him. Here's my phone number."

That very night we brought Snuffy home with us to Faith Tabernacle where we was staying. He told us later he thought we was running some kind of a con game at first, 'cause we was all running around the place with Bibles under our arms. And there was one boy who was down on his knees praying all the time.

The Devil was messing with Snuffy for quite a while, but we took him around to churches with us where we went to sing and tell about the power of the Lord in our lives. And we prayed for him. We knew he was a tough one; but we all were, you know, so we just expected God would have to do a miracle for Snuffy too.

17. Little Joe

When Little Joe came to Christ he felt free for the first time in his life. His friend's mother had been talking about Damascus Church for a long time, but Joey didn't want to hear about it before. Now, he was real skinny, and his back hurt, and he felt so sick all the time that he quit his job. He was up tight, and he called her up and asked if she would make an appointment for him.

Two days later he came to the church with his clothes, and after kicking his habit a few days, he went on up to Mountaindale. All the guys talked to him and prayed with him, and it was all strange to Joe, but very real. He told me later,

"I used to sit in the back at the meetings, and it was really funny to me the way you all were praising God. But I couldn't make fun of you guys."

Then one morning after he'd been there two weeks, the Bible teacher asked if anyone wanted to accept the Saviour. Joe was ready, so he raised his hand, and then walked on up to the front with several other boys. The teacher asked Joe to pray after him, but all Joey could say was,

"Lord, Lord. Talk to me. Talk to me. Talk to me."

And while he was standing there crying, he heard God saying to him,

"Joe, all this time I've been looking upon you, waiting for you to turn to Me."

Joe told us,

"I felt a power coming up through my feet, up through my legs—all through me. I was free. I started praying with beautiful words, and I looked at myself wondering, 'Is this me? What am I saying?' I felt like I was completely free from everything. For the first time the power that had held me all my life was fallen away. I had used God's name so often without even thinking about it, and here He was so real now. I was so free, so happy; and I was afraid to get off my knees 'cause I'd never had such an experience, and I didn't want it to end. The joy tears just ran down my face! Everyone left and I kneeled there, asking God to stay with me."

Five years earlier Little Joe was just standing on the corner in the Bronx with four of his buddies, when this guy came along with a bag of heroin. He gave them all a sniff; it was kind of like an accident. But they all got hooked.

All his life something had held Joe back. He didn't have no will power. Everything he cared to do always came out wrong. He could never talk to nobody. Drugs, he discovered, made him act very silly, and he liked that "who cares" feeling. Whenever he tried to get away from drugs he was always sad or bored. He felt such an emptiness like he couldn't stand still — like he needed to be somewhere else, worrying about something.

One Sunday night, breaking through a jewelry store window, Little Joe almost bled to death. When his folks came to the hospital, Joe promised them he would never use drugs again. But as soon as he got out of the hospital and went home to say hello to his mother, he headed around the block to a basement "shooting" gallery. Right away he took a shot, even though he knew it might react badly with the drugs he had in the hospital. Joe didn't care much about living.

Even as a little kid, then later when he was using drugs, Joe would lay in bed and ask, "Why did I come into this life? What has this world got to offer me? I never done nothing right. Why am I this way? Why do I have to do all these things? Why drugs and drunks and trouble and gangs — like the world's a disappointment? Why? Why am I living?"

We all knew that Joe had never been able to talk very well with anyone. Yet that morning at Mountaindale we heard him ask God for forgiveness of all his sins and we saw him kneel there for hours, just praising and thanking God. And from that day on we could see how Little Joe was completely delivered from drugs, from drinking, from smoking — from everything that had bound him up tight. He used to be so nervous he'd just be walking, walking, walking. That all left him.

"I didn't know anything about God," he explained. "As far as I was concerned, God was up there and I was down here, and God couldn't do nothin' for me. I was so wrong."

Joe went home and told his parents; and right away he started helping his brother who was a glue sniffer—a glue addict. He got him up to Mountaindale, and he got changed by the power of God too.

"Now I know why I'm living," Joe tells everybody. "In New York I never saw the love of God — even your best friend would stick a knife in your back. But the love of God makes us love other people—not because they've done something for us, but because the love of God just flows."

18. Juggy

With some guys it's tougher. It took five times at the camp before Juggy made it. He didn't think he could ever serve God; he just didn't think God would ever pick up a guy like him. This was a miracle in itself.

When Juggy accepted the Lord he was fooling around, but evidently God wasn't. Juggy just wanted to get away from himself; he didn't really have any intention of getting down to business. He couldn't even imagine such a thing. He wanted to leave dope. Period. He was not interested in changing anything else. He didn't think he could make it without this pleasure, or that one. Women were hard to leave, dancing, drinking.

Juggy was born in the Bronx, and he was only three years old when his Puerto Rican mother separated from her Irish husband. He was the only child and he was always out in the street 'cause there wasn't anybody to play with in the house. His mother worked off and on, and Juggy got in the habit of keeping things to himself.

School was just fooling around. But the grades he occasionally brought home showed that Juggy could have done a good job if the world had been a little kinder to him. When the school would send those yellow cards home through the mail, Juggy would open up the mailbox and tear them up so his Mom never seen them. By the time she found out and went to school to the dean's office, Juggy'd been skipping school a couple months.

"I used to get up early," Juggy says, "and take my books and run up the stairs to the skylight and ditch the books on the roof. Then I'd jump to the next roof and come down through another building. Across the street the fellows would be waiting for me, and we'd go to a candy store and get some cigarettes and listen to records in the juke box."

When he did go to school he would cut most of the classes. The only one he enjoyed was drawing class — he used to sketch. Liked music and basketball — stuff like that. Everything else he didn't care much for. By sixth grade he was playing hookey, fighting in gangs, and being sent to youth houses and reformatories upstate. Life was a pretty big puzzle.

Juggy spent a lot of time in the pool room—used to shoot pool in the night time. Then he started dancing—Latin American dancing—and playing Conga drums. He took off from school to get a job, but instead he started selling marijuana. Sometimes he'd buy it bagged already. A five dollar bag was maybe fifteen sticks. Make a dollar on a bag; have a couple guys working for him.

"I was living by myself," Juggy says, "and I used to get up early in the morning and smoke, in the afternoon smoke, in the evening smoke, night time smoke, all night smoke. And I was just smokin', smokin', smokin' away till there came a time when I wasn't ever sober. Regular cigarettes and pot. I was so high I couldn't really tell how many pot."

You know if you're smokin' in a small room—maybe two or three guys burning this pot—it just fills the whole room with smoke. You get twisted outa your mind. You're so high you don't know what you're doing. We used to burn our clothes with a cigarette, and we wouldn't even know it. We'd talk about everything: what we were gonna do that day, how good the marijuana was, or who we got it from. The kick was just laughing and carrying on. Just sitting there was a good feeling. A gay type of feeling.

This friend of Juggy's used to play in bands and they would go to one of these Spanish lodges upstate for the weekend. There'd be dancing, music — mambos, boleros. He was real addicted to pot — staying high on pot all the time. Juggy used to sit in the bandstand with him, and just get high too. Pick up a stray girl and stay with her for the weekend — just for pleasure. It was expected. He never got serious.

Friday night is always a big night in the Bronx. No one can sit home on a Friday night. Everything's moving, especially after nine o'clock. The girls are out on the boulevard; there's a lot more money on Friday night. Some of them wait all day for a special "trick" who comes to the Bronx just on weekends.

This is the night to get dressed up and go out — to a movie or a dance. People come out on the stoop and get into a car and drive off. And if you don't have the money or a date, you hang out the window and whistle or make cracks at the neighbors who've got it better this week. Or maybe your shoulders sag a little further as you watch. Like the little woman who ain't been out in months. Her husband comes home, kicks his shoes off, opens up a six-pack of beer and settles in front of the television.

"Hurry up with supper, Jane," he calls, taking her for granted. "I'm beat." She's tired too, but she's given up expecting much out of life. Later she'll join the grandmas next door, and the junkie on four, and the little girl with her baby, and they'll sit on the stoop in the heavy summer night and talk about who got busted today and who's getting out of jail next month and what Rita was wearing tonight and what number came out at 5:30 . . . .

Sometimes Juggy and his friends would gather in the hall and pool their money for wine. After the trip to the liquor store they would sit on their stoop and sip the wine until they got warmed up enough to start singing. They liked to sing inside the hallway 'cause of the echo. Then they'd get out the marijuana, and smoke and sip and sing. Juggy says they tried to crash the Ted Mack Amateur Hour one time, but they were so stoned they didn't know what they were doing.

"Other times three or four of us guys would get all sharped up on a Friday night. We'd smoke some pot and drink some wine. Then about nine o'clock we'd get a cab and shoot downtown to a dance. There'd be maybe 250 people there. The guys would chip in and we'd get a setup table with a bottle of whiskey and ginger ale and all that. We'd drink and get up and walk around the dance hall and meet different people. See a nice looking girl, and we'd be high, so we'd just introduce ourselves, start talking. I'd talk to this one; my friend would talk to another one. Before you know it we'd join the tables and have a ball all night. Once in a while we'd sneak away; go into the bathroom and light up a joint. Come back and sip some whiskey and talk.

"It would cost us at least sixty or seventy dollars, but we were like in the business — selling this marijuana, making enough profit between us to take care of a night like that."

That was the way to enjoy yourself — Friday, Saturday, Sunday. Juggy was a real swinger! He thought he was really living! He had no idea of changing anything else about his life. Only dope he wanted to get away from.

The first time Juggy went to Mountaindale he stayed three weeks and then ran away. He hitch-hiked 90 miles back to New York City, and it was cold. When he got to the city about nine o'clock at night, he got some money together, and bought a bottle of wine. After he drunk the wine his mind was all messed up, so he went out and bought a bag of dope. He still had his Bible from camp, and he put the dope inside the Bible and walked down the avenue with the Bible under his arm. High on alcohol, with a Bible fronting for the dope, Juggy stopped to borrow this guy's works.

He knew dope and alcohol don't mix, but he figured his resistance was high—three weeks away, he couldn't be that clean yet. He took off on the roof—only half a bag of dope, but this dope was dynamite. And he fell out. Thank God there was a guy with him. He beat Juggy half to death up there trying to revive him. He gave him three salt injections to counteract the heroin. And he finally brought him around after Juggy'd been out for more than three hours. Juggy's face was all puffed up as he came to and asked,

"What happened?"

It was real late—maybe three o'clock in the morning, and he was lying there all stretched out. This was after he had really made a vow to God; and the first thing that came to his mind was this: God spared my life!

The next time he was at camp he came back to the city on a pass; he was up on the rooftop with this guy and a girl taking off. A cop came and he had a gun. This girl was about ready to take off when Juggy seen the gun, so he yelled, "Hold it!" A shot went off, and the girl screamed, and he was sure the cop had shot her. This was a narco and he searched everybody. Juggy had picked up the needle and the eye dropper and throwed all that over the roof; but the cop found a tract in Juggy's pocket that said, "God can do it!"

"What's this?" he asked.

"I'm trying to make it over at this church—Damasco." Juggy told him how he was a drug addict, but he wasn't really addicted then 'cause he'd been up at this camp. He told him he was on a pass and would be going back to Mountaindale soon. The narco let him go. Juggy could have got busted; he could have got shot. But we believe it was God again. We see the hand of God so much in our lives. Juggy wasn't changed yet, but he'd heard enough of the Word to have the faith that God was taking care of him.

He knew that God was doing something with his life, and he started getting interested in the Bible. It didn't come as just a sudden thing, but every day was another step, and something was changing his life. All the funny old desires he thought he couldn't live without started to leave him. One night at Mountaindale—this was the fifth time he was back to camp — Juggy accepted the Lord. He used to mock faith, scorn it, laugh about it, criticize it — did everything in the book about it. But all the time he would feel that it had to be real. He knew for a dope addict to really change it took power—and lots of it. Juggy got down on his knees that night and prayed,

"God, if this is the power I need I want it. You know how weak I am. If You gotta gift for me, more than what You already give me—well, I want it. What's keeping me from it?"

God must have seen sincerity in Juggy and He let him have it. It was a complete cleansing. He was light as a feather — felt like he could float upstairs. He was in a daze, another world, another realm—the realm of the Spirit of God. Then the words in the Bible started to be enlightening; everything became alive. Singing came alive; witnessing for Christ came alive. It wasn't a duty telling people about Christ. He felt life.

You know, we'd never make it if testifying was just a duty anyway. When you been dead, it's not hard to know that you're alive now! God honored Juggy's desire on a Friday. He was changed overnight. He went into New York to the church on Saturday, and he was talking to guys upstairs in the dormitory. He was praying for the sick; he was doing everything in the book. The people there looked at Juggy and said,

"Him? Preaching?" Juggy'd been the talk of the place for a while; some of the guys was afraid there was no help for Juggy — even in church.

"Looks like the same man, but it ain't the same man at all!" they said.

19. The Mystery of God

The whole eight months I was at Mountaindale I was always getting ready to leave the place. Not that I didn't like it. But even after I was converted, and feeling great, I was always in some kind of controversy. God had to chop away at me, bringing me some patience and wisdom and love. I was so rebellious, you know; it was just my nature.

After I had been back and forth several times between Damascus Church in the Bronx, and the camp, I got into one particularly tremendous trial. Brother Keller called me a Pharisee, an accuser of the brethren, and put me up before the entire congregation. That really knocked away a big chunk of my pride that day. I had a great desire to purge anything that was bad in the camp. I figured if a guy does wrong, he can't stay here. I forgot already that Christ came to seek and to save those that were lost—and that I was one of that kind such a short time ago. I didn't realize what I was doing. I thought I was right. I didn't want this camp destroyed—I didn't want nobody to hurt it; and I thought this guy was hurting it. He was a guy I brought there myself; I had led him to the Lord in the church; and his conduct at Mountaindale hurt me bad. I thought he was doing a lot of harm; but the people at Mountaindale were determined to help him; and I couldn't understand them. So they dealt with me before the entire group. This was just a couple days before Christmas, and I was supposed to have the Christmas service. But I got my suitcase out and packed it and took off down the road.

A car came along and stopped. Reverend Keller and a couple of boys jumped out, saying,

"Come on, Johnny! Come on back."

"No, I'm not going back there. I don't need that; I can make it on my own."

They knew it wouldn't do any good to try to talk me into it; but after they left I was scared. I knew I couldn't make it on my own. I looked up at the sky and said,

"God, if You want me back, send somebody to stop me." And I kept right on walking down the road toward the city.

Boy! It wasn't ten minutes till I heard this car coming, and the most unlikely messenger from God steps out. Now this guy—he never showed any emotion for anybody, and he used to get me mad the way he'd kid around about the things of God, 'cause I was jealous for God, and this guy really bothered me.

When I saw him coming toward me, I thought, "Certainly *he* wasn't sent from God!" But God does those things—this was one of the "foolish things" He uses to confound us. And as I looked at him the tears began to fall down his face, and he said,

"Please, Johnny, don't go! You know God don't want you to go. You know what will happen if you leave. Please stay. The guys, they look up to ya."

WOW! I just stood there looking down at the road, saying,

"Thank you, Lord! Thank you!" I knew it was God bringing me home.

I got in the car and rode back with him, and went up to my room to pray. After that, the next day was Christmas, and I just abandoned myself to God for that service: "Go ahead, Lord. Go ahead!"

There must have been close to a hundred visitors there. I felt like a pipe with the cold clear water running through it. Sometimes it's like myself stands away and looks back at me; and I feel as though God is pushing words through my mind and out through my mouth. God just blessed the service in such a great way. And I couldn't stop crying. When I get blessed, really strong in God, I cry. I weep and I weep.

Some time later I was still in conflict with Brother Keller. He played a tremendous part in my life—the Kellers were the directors of the camp at that time. I was walking down the hall, and here comes Brother Keller walking towards me. Now I wouldn't even say hello to him, 'cause I was still mad. I'd pucker up like a little kid—stick my lip out. Mean! But he stopped me and said,

"Johnny, you're preaching tomorrow."

Sunday morning? Nobody but the head man ever preaches on Sunday morning—or somebody he has the utmost confidence in. This was the main service. I looked at him and I felt strange. Right away in my mind I say, "What is he trying to do? Make me look like a fool? I'm no preacher, I know this. I can talk, but I can't preach."

So I turned around and went into Sister Matthews' house. She and her husband were from India, and I called her "Mama." Anything I'd ask her she'd say, "Let's look in the Bible." And God would always give us the word.

When I walked in I told her,

"You know, Reverend Keller just told me to preach tomorrow."

"Well, praise the Lord!"

"But, Mama Matthews, you know I can't preach. Maybe he wants to make a fool out of me."

"Don't worry. It isn't you, Johnny; let God do the preaching."

I looked at her with that *thing* in the way—that *self* in there, and I said,

"What am I gonna preach about?"

"Look in the Bible, Johnny."

So I sat there at the table reading the Bible for a long time, and I told Mama,

"I still don't know!"

"Well, Johnny, there is no doubt in my mind that the Spirit will tell you what to do. Why don't you go to sleep now, and set your alarm for about 6 o'clock in the morning?"

I thanked her and went on up to my room, and set the clock for seven—figured I'd get an extra hour of sleep. Six o'clock's a ridiculous time for anybody to get up—especially if you don't have to! I was sleeping and all of a sudden I thought I heard like a voice calling,

"Johnny! Johnny!"

I opened my eyes, and I knew exactly, immediately what it was—like my body was responding to the Spirit of God all around me. I got up and put my clothes on, and started walking out as though someone were leading me by the hand. It was just coming light as we walked out of the building and down the road. When we got out away from the camp, I kneeled down to pray.

The sun was coming up. There was this blue, and a darker blue, and a gray; then there was orange and yellow, and I saw all this. Did you ever watch an artist mixing colors to get the right combination? It was like God was playing a color symphony for me—showing me all this beauty, stroke by stroke, note by note. Especially for Johnny Gimenez. God was putting into play all His great artistic majesty. Everything was just so good, and as I watched I felt as though I became separated. Someone was calling, "Come, come."

I felt my spirit leaving—going up, up to the skies, and there I saw Jesus standing, waiting for me. As I came close I could see the prints on His hands, and He had such a beautiful smile on His face, as though He had known me all my life and was so delighted I had finally come.

He grabbed my hand and we started walking. He was leading me over the skies, like from star to star. And all of a sudden He said,

"Johnny, I'm going to show you Creation! Look!"

And as I looked I saw the earth. It was like a plot of land, and as I watched, Blup! a blade of grass just popped out of the earth.

Then He said, "Look!"

And I saw a tree, and the buds opened up.

And He said, "Look!"

And I seen the baby of a deer laying down under the tree, and he opened one big eye and looked at me.

One after another God led me to fields, to mountains, to the sea. Along the shore I saw the fish eggs, and a little fish come out. And then, a chick and a rabbit and an elephant — one by one I seen these animals coming to life. Then I seen Adam laying there and God said,

"Look!"

Like a big wind swept over him, and Adam opened his eyes and looked at God. Then another wind blew a cloud over him, and when I looked back he was laying there with Eve beside him.

From the Garden of Eden He led me to the mountain, and I saw Moses with the commandments in stone, and God said to me,

"Read!"

And I read the commandments, one by one, right off the tablets of stone.

Then He led me to Gideon. Gideon was coming with his great army—the best men in all Israel, and God looked at me and smiled and said,

"There is no match anywhere, because besides having this great band of men, he has Me." You remember how He talked to Gideon? "You have too many men. You have too many!"

He kept on and on through the Bible, till one of the greatest things He showed me—

"Look!"

And I saw John, the beloved disciple, leaning on the heart of Christ, like he was listening to a telephone, and I could hear,

"Love, love, love, love, love." And I could see the heartbeat: love-love-love-love-love-love-love.

And He showed me the cross, and the cross was like in the heart, and the whole thing was pulsing: LOVE-LOVE-LOVE-LOVE. And this heartbeat was like swooping all over the world. The first disciples were thrust out with the pulsing of God's heart, and they preached that Christ is love, and love is Christ. And the whole ministry before me showed me that the most important thing of all is LOVE. How God loves the world! Man!

He ran me all the way through Revelation and He showed me millions and millions and millions of hearts, and He said,

"Look!"

And I saw hearts, nothing but hearts. And this big giant hand—knocking, knocking, knocking. Knocking at all the hearts.

Then I became aware of the roadside again, and the tree over me and the sun higher in the sky. And I got up from my knees and it was service time. Three hours had passed; the guys had eaten breakfast, and they were already in the service, singing.

I didn't want to come back from being up there with Him, but I knew in my mind that God had done this for me for this particular day. I walked into the service, and fell on my knees while they were singing. I was weeping, and I asked,

"Lord, why *me?* Why did you choose me? Why?"

I felt that God had singled me out, and I felt so insignificant, so small. Why me? Dirty, filthy sinner—Johnny Gimenez. And I kept crying and praying there on my knees, and everybody in the place began to sense the presence of God's Spirit. I could feel the power building and building. Guys were singing and speaking in tongues and praising the Lord.

After they introduced me I remember getting up, with so much emotion, and I just said very simply,

"God has just showed me Creation! And the text He gave me is from the first chapter of Genesis, verse 2: 'The Spirit of the Lord moved upon the waters.' "

Right away everybody sensed it. They could see it happening; they weren't hearing words — they were *looking,* seeing the Spirit of the Lord moving upon the waters, and upon the waters of their own souls at that very moment. And before I knew it, God was giving us a great visitation of His Spirit. Some of the boys started coming up to the altar, and they were all weeping to the Lord. Some were repenting, some were thanking God, some were praising the Lord. I felt like a little baby taken into a great mystery of God.

20. Frankie

After Frankie came to Damascus, one of the first things he had to face up to was his parole. Mom Rosado, our "mother in Christ," helped so many of us boys find the way to God. Frankie was always the moving kind. And he was always in trouble with the law—all of us were. The cops knew us well.

As we look back we can see a lot of little things that turned us off from the mark. Like stealing that pencil from the kid in the third grade, or swiping doughnuts out of the bakery truck, or playing hookey and lying about where we spent the day. Little things we felt convicted about but shied away from in our minds. We been punished many times by teachers, and principals, and truant officers. After that it's Children's Court. Then training school, detention home, reformatory.

Frankie got busted for panhandling — begging nickels and dimes on the street; for boosting — going into the stores and shoplifting. He'd get clothes all kinds of ways. Like some lady would hang a pair of pants on the clothesline, and if they fit Frankie, they goes on him. Shirts too. He would go into a store and try on some clothes. He put on the store clothes then he'd put his own clothes on top of theirs and walk out. When he was hungry, here comes the bakery truck. He walks by and WHOOSH! bread and doughnuts for the morning. He ran away from the Catholic orphanage when he was 13 — started living on the rooftops, pickpocketing people in the subways, entering apartments through fire escapes, open windows; started smoking pot when he was 14; went eight times to jail.

Frankie was always alone. His mother died on the operating table in Puerto Rico when he was born. He never has found his father. Many times on the rooftops he used to look down at the people and try to think what his mother's face was like. When he'd burglarize an apartment, he'd sit down inside and play it was his house. And he'd wonder what it would be like to have his own keys in his pocket, and to walk in the front door and go to bed in a real bed—his own bed. He still wonders, "If I'd had a mother, or a father, would I have fell into dope?"

Frankie had always felt so much jealousy because he didn't have no family of his own. He used to see mothers looking for their sons, and he kept wondering what it would be like to have someone who cared for him. The only ones he could say was his mother and father was the addicts he knew.

He and Lennie used to look out for each other. Mostly when an addict gets a bag it's for himself; but Lennie used to get a bag and he'd start looking for Frankie. Then they'd sit down and shoot the bag together. And when Frankie would beg or steal nickels and dimes, he would buy bread and coffee for Lennie. When he would be going someplace to get himself clean he would make sure to bring Lennie with him. They did all kinds of things together.

Then Lennie got busted and went to jail, and Frankie got busted on a different charge, and they met in Riker's Island. They had lots of time to sit back and talk. Lennie was going on parole first, and he was plotting a nice big stick-up job when he got out so he could buy enough dope to get back to pushing. They talked about some things they would pull together when Frankie got out too.

About a month and a half after Lennie went on parole, Frankie saw his number 465089 on the mail call board. The inmates were kidding him because he never had nobody to write letters to him.

"Hey, Frankie! Somebody wrote to you? Did you write to yourself?"

He didn't know how to read; it was too tough. So he took it back to the block and gave it to one of the inmates to read to him.

"Frankie, I'm sorry that the plans we had have to be broken, but like I'm a Christian now. The Lord took me over and I'm a new person."

Frankie thought the man must be reading through the lines, so he told him to read it twice. Like what happened here? Maybe Lennie's trying to tell me something. But that's all there was.

Frankie had only a couple more months to do in the prison. When he first got out he looked for Lennie but couldn't find him so he went right back to begging nickels and dimes. And the very same day he left Riker's Island he took a shot of dope. He had learned a trade in the prison; he could sew. But he didn't even try to get a job. He went back to the street and got worse than he was before. He didn't report in to his parole officer like he should once or twice a week, so the police were after him.

But one day Lennie's cousin told Frankie that he ought to go over to the Damascus Church because Lennie was back from camp. When he went inside they told him Lennie was upstairs. Frankie saw him kneeling down, so he walked over and watched him until he finally looked up. Lennie jumped up and they grabbed each other:

"Frankie, you know something? I was just praying for you at this moment! I know you won't believe it, but I was. And I got sixty boys in that camp praying for you—that God would just bring you to me, or me to you. And He brought you! Frankie, I want just five minutes of your time."

Frankie gave him a queer look. He needed dope, so he told him,

"Man! I'm sick."

"Look, Frankie, just five minutes?"

They started arguing and pushing each other and Frankie said,

"Leave me alone, Lennie, or I'll punch you in the mouth. Let me go, hear?"

But Lennie just kept on crying and showing him the Bible:

"Look, Frankie, I found the way. There IS a way out, Frankie. I found it, and you can too."

Frankie pushed him away so hard that he fell to the floor, but Lennie recovered and grabbed onto his legs and told him,

"I never gonna let you go, Frankie! You can kick me. You can bite me. You can do anything you want, but I'm not gonna let you go."

Frankie looked down at him and said, "Man, what do you want?"

"Just five minutes."

You know, when you look down and a person you like an awful lot looks up into your eyes, crying like a real baby, something happens inside of you. So Frankie said,

"OK, Lennie, I'm gonna stay for five minutes."

"Listen, Frankie, God done it for me. I'm not the same guy I was before."

Right away Frankie could tell that it wasn't Lennie speaking—even before he told him about the new spirit that he had. He knew something pretty serious had happened to his best buddy. For the whole five minutes he looked right into Lennie's eyes. But he'd been taken so many times in his life that he had to say,

"Lennie, don't you fool me!" Even though he knew Lennie had to be telling the truth.

"Frankie, if this was a game I'd tell you; but it's not. You gonna walk out them doors with your head up. You don't want anybody to call you dirty Frankie no more. God can do it for you, too."

Frankie got down on his knees beside Lennie, and said, "God, if it's true what Lennie says, let me have this new spirit. Let me kick this habit if it's true I don't have to be a junkie anymore. I don't know what's the meaning or what's the feeling of somebody to love me. But I want to know."

After Frankie came to Christ one of the things that bothered him was how he hadn't kept his parole. Mom Rosado and I took Frankie downtown to the big building which is the city headquarters for all paroles. Right away they grabbed Frankie and threw him up against the wall and started searching him. Frankie finally told them he'd come to give himself up, and Mom was explaining to the parole officer, but he talked so snotty that she got mad and demanded she be taken to the parole commissioner.

The commissioner said he would see her, so she went in to present Frankie's case, but she went by herself. When he was ready to talk to Frankie, he had everything down to a simple formula,

"Frank," he said, "I got just three words for you. One, don't you dare go back on dope. Two, you stay in that church with Mrs. Rosado. Three, don't you ever give me no more trouble."

And that's just what they got in Frankie. He kept reporting back to the parole officer until he had a chance to leave the city. At that time he went back to ask permission and they gave it to them.

"Thank you, sir." Frankie could scarcely believe what was happening.

"I hope you make it, Frank," the officer said to him.

"Mr. G., if it was me, you'd still be looking for me, but I'm changed now. God done it. Not me."

"Wow! You've changed a lot, Frank. You've showed me another way. There's two ways, I guess. I get them out of the street and put them in jail; you're taking them out of the street and bringing them to God."

Frankie laughed and said, "I think my way's the best! I been in jail eight times and nothing like this ever happened to me!"

I believe that God saved Lennie so that Frankie would listen to him for that five minutes. If it had been anybody else who come to talk about God, Frankie would just have pushed them off:

"Yeah, OK. Later, man, later. Yeah, yeah, yeah."

21. Terry

Terry had everything he needed as he grew up—except the recognition, acceptance, tolerance which he desperately wanted. His father was a dark Negro. His mother was light-complexioned, daughter of a Castilian Spanish matriarch who owned slaves. Terry was born dark, and all the years we knew him in the Bronx he was out to prove something. The rebelliousness inside him made him the terror of the block. Dope was the only relief he knew from the hatred he felt for himself and everybody else.

Terry moved with his mother to the Bronx when he was seven years old. His father had already left a couple years before that, and his mother and grandmother and sister and him moved several times after the divorce.

"My mother was only 25," Terry says. "She was young and she had needs that only a man could fulfill. So she got a boyfriend. I didn't understand this. He'd come live with us Saturdays and Sundays — raised me up. But I started criticizing and judging my own mother. I loved my father very much, and I used to go out and search for him till I found him.

"My grandmother—she's Castilian and had slaves. She used to tell me, 'Your father's black and no good!' But one day when I was 11 years old I answered her back, 'Grandma, do you love me? I look just like my father.' She never let me forget the difference and all the hate in me started right there in my own family. My sister and I grew up very close to each other. We always stood in the corner by ourselves, and my family would look over at me and say, 'You look like an inkspot.' "

Terry was brought up in the Catholic Church. He made his confirmation, his communion. "They gave me a Bible," Terry recalls, "when I was ten years old. I didn't know what it was, but I kept it. And I remember for a long time I'd go to sleep with it right next to my cheek. It got all sweat through 'cause I slept with it so much. And I would say my own little prayers as I lay there in the dark."

Off and on during those early years he would see his father at his grandfather's parties. But it was just a sort of "Hi, Pop, gimme a dollar," and that was it. Never did things with him. Never saw a baseball game till he was twenty. Still never been to a football game. Used to look at his friends when they went with their dads, and felt like crying. One day when he was about twelve and a half he played hookey from the Bronx school and he just happened to meet his father on the street. He was so glad to see him that he wanted to embrace him. But his father hit him because he was playing hookey:

"Terry, I want you to be better than me. We gonna talk man-to-man."

But Terry wanted him to love him, and after that day he agreed with his grandma—that his father was no good.

Love was one word that meant something very much to him. Now he can see that there was love in his family, but then he couldn't understand it. He had too much fear in him. So he just drew back from them. Finally when he was 14 he jumped up and told his family,

"You're a bunch of hypocrites. You talk about how you love each other and yet you're always gossiping. There's no love in this house."

They tried their best, but they tried to say, "I love you" materially—by giving him things. So he learned no value for things 'cause he always had them.

Growing up in a Jewish neighborhood, he became very color conscious. He started gang fighting with the guys in his block. They were all right. They told him, "You can hang out." Then he'd go into a party, and feel this tension inside as he walked in.

Nobody said anything, but he'd feel it just as sure as if they said, "What's he doin' here?"

Then he'd think, "OK, I'm gonna mess up this party." He knew what he could do. He knew he wasn't going to get beat. He'd walk over and ask a girl,

"Would you care to dance?"

And she'd say, "No."

Automatically he'd ask, "Why? Because I'm colored?"

And she'd say, "No, I just don't want to."

"Well, let's dance then."

By now he'd want to start a fight, and he'd keep it up till the other guys would take a poke at him and the party would end in a riot.

Later he'd speak to his sister about what happened and she'd tell him, "Terry, you don't do things like that!" And he'd ask her why.

"Well, girls are girls; they're not like you."

After that he started breaking down, and he had six or seven girl friends. But he didn't really know how to act with them. Then he went away at sixteen — got arrested for the Sullivan law — pistol-whipped somebody because of discrimination. That's when he started thinking—really thinking. Learned to live by his wits. And he figured out a lot of things about people—found out how to *use* them. And he went with many kinds of women until he was nineteen. Then he went to live with a woman who was twenty-seven and he grew up. Living with a woman is like a school.

Terry found that "little things mean a lot to a woman; it's not the sexual. A pat or a kiss while she's cooking, picking something up to please her, letting her know you like the way she's wearing her hair, knowing how to talk with her. I learned how to build her up to love, and we both could enjoy it. I found out you can't turn on an emotion, 'cause a person is not a machine."

But all the time he was trying to prove something. And in the rebelliousness and the fighting inside of him he would shoot people, stab people, cut people up—sometimes for no reason. And then he would cry because he had to buy his own friends. Everybody was afraid of Terry. He used to stick up the dope pushers for their dope—kidnapped one of the guys one time and took him away. He was just an animal. He didn't care. He didn't like his own kind, and he didn't like himself. He didn't like no one. His fear built a wall. And he figured if he could put enough fear into you, you wouldn't bother him. He learned two things early: either you gave it to him, or he took it. Fear was a powerful weapon, and he knew how to use it, what he could do with it. And yet many times people would look at Terry and say,

"Terry, you're not like that." And a big wall would come down, and he'd snap back, "What do you mean?"

Terry was an angry man; he was in and out of jail. He was not easy to live with. He did everything possible for so long to have no one get close to him. But in this woman he found some of the love he was searching for. This was a case where two people grew together. Terry and Phyllis were learning to think about each other, not just *use* each other.

When Terry was about twenty, he decided he wanted to get a "vacation with pay," so he worked as a mail clerk in a store just off Fifth Avenue, and he did well. They trusted him to deliver money to the bank and everything. He had clothes and money, but something was still missing in life. When he got his vacation with pay, he went to Puerto Rico with his mother and sister and quit his job. There Terry seen his grandfather on his mother's side, and the first thing he heard him say to his daughter—after twenty-five years was,

"Those kids belong to a colored man, right?"

After they returned to New York, Terry was living in the Bowery, and drinking wine with the men down there. One night he got shot in the leg. People figured, "This'll stop him now." He put too much fear in everybody. That's what happened with this boy who shot him. Terry told him, "The next time I see you I'm gonna kill you!" So he was just too scared and the next time he seen Terry he shot him.

In the hospital, Phyllis went to see him and she said,

"Terry, what are you gonna do?"

He was thinking of putting a pistol in his hand and going out to shoot the boy because he shot him. But Phyllis said to him,

"You're not going to shoot the boy, Terry, because of what people might say of you?"

You see, she knew he was living for something that he wasn't. People would expect him to do the violent, the hateful thing. This was his reputation. But she helped him to see that he wasn't what they thought he was. And he didn't shoot him. He accepted the fact, "I bleed just like anybody else. I'm really no different." And he started relaxing.

In 1961 Phyllis gave birth to a little girl, and Terry started working again. He figured, "Now I have somebody I can love." But he was afraid of the baby. He became very self-sufficient. He could cook, wash diapers, run the sewing machine, knit. He didn't really need no one—he had himself all built up. But he was still afraid to love the baby. He was afraid to get that tight with anyone. He would get close, but once he felt you knew him, he would draw back.

* * *

After Terry had been addicted ten years his mother got very tired and weary. Her nerves had got so bad that she had been taking sleeping pills to rest for two years. Terry was in the streets and knew little of the trouble that was crowding her into a corner.

It was Christmas. Terry and Phyllis and the baby came into her house thinking this would be a happy day in the middle of a whole string of empty ones. They looked forward to the cheer of the Christmas spirit to bring everybody together at least for a few hours. But as they walked in the door Terry's mother grabbed his hand and said,

"Terry, I know how you feel now. I feel great."

Everybody in the house looked gruesome. She had taken an overdose of sleeping pills. And this man that was living with her had given her some coffee which just exploded the pills more. She wobbled over to her purse and took out some money and handed it to Terry,

"Here's ten dollars, Terry. Let's go buy some dope and get high—just you and I."

She said it very secretly, "Just you and I. We'll be together. Now I know how you feel."

There was such a bottomless feeling in Terry's heart. He didn't even have any real thoughts; he just shook his head — this kind of thing would not come to his mother!

"Ma, please don't. Please don't."

He knew he ought to say, "Ma, I love you," but he didn't feel it. He didn't know what he felt. When his Grandma came over and said, "It's all your fault, Terry," everything inside him rebelled.

"No, it is not my fault, Grandma. You never loved any of us. It's your fault!"

And he ran out the door and stuck somebody up for dope. Before Christmas Day dragged out, Terry stuck up several people. He hoped one of them would give him a fight that might end his life.

A few months later an argument over something that cost fifty cents almost did cost Terry his life. It was one o'clock in the afternoon and everybody was out in the streets. This guy wouldn't give Terry what he wanted, so they both pulled knives and Terry stabbed the man, and in turn he got a long gash across the right side of his abdomen.

Four friends came running up to help the other guy, "What happened?"

Terry grabbed them and asked, "What do you guys want?"

They panicked, "Whatsa matter with this guy? Has he gone nuts?" And they ran and got a garbage can lid, a baseball bat, a broken bottle.

All of them came at Terry and started fighting him. He turned to one side and got cut in the back of the neck; he turned to the other side and punched one of them. When he went to pick up a piece of pipe he stumbled and fell, and the guys hit him over the head with the baseball bat and the garbage can lid and they stomped on his back as hard as they could. They were out to kill him. The people who had been staring suddenly turned and disappeared. The gang of five left too, and Terry pulled himself up and began walking. He didn't care what happened to himself, but he was ready to kill somebody. For ten and a half hours he walked through the Bronx. He stuck somebody else up; actually he was looking for a pistol to kill somebody. But he began to feel so faint that he finally went into a hospital. They told him he was bleeding internally and had been losing blood for a number of hours. When they operated they had to remove one of his kidneys and for several days he remained on the critical list.

His mother came to the hospital right away and stayed with him. She didn't want him to tell anyone that he was an addict. So nobody knew what was happening as he came out of anesthesia. When he came to, he found all these tubes in his nose and his arms and he was having all the symptoms of withdrawal. He was so dry inside he couldn't stand it. He yanked the tubes out of his nose and grabbed the pan under his bed and drank the liquid in it. The nurse came in the door and saw what was happening; she went white as a sheet and screamed,

"God Almighty, man! What are you doing? You're not supposed to drink anything!" And she ran out of the room.

Almost immediately two doctors appeared and Terry told them he had to have some medication 'cause he was an addict.

"Why didn't you tell us before?" They ordered morphine for him first, and then explained to him that if he'd tried to go on through withdrawal without any medication, he would have died. The terrible heaving, they said, would have torn him loose inside and he surely would have bled to death.

Three weeks after major surgery Terry was back on the street addicted to morphine. He knew no other way. For eleven years he had been searching and probing and never finding an answer. He was tired. He never expected to live. He didn't want to live. He was lost.

One day Phyllis said, "Terry, why don't you go to church?"

He looked at her like she was crazy. "If I go to church you and I may never be together again."

"You go!" she said.

They had learned to communicate, and one of the most beautiful things in the world is to communicate, to be able to express. To say "I don't like this" or "I like that." To talk it out, and not hold it back. You know how I feel and I know how you feel. When you have this fair exchange, you have something beautiful. Terry and Phyllis had found this and they could help each other.

So he went over to Damascus, and his first impression was "Who can I stick up here?"

But he asked God one thing: "If you're real, God, teach me how to love. Teach me how to care for people."

And God did this for Terry. The most fantastic thing—you can't even explain it. He found God had forgiven him, and he repented. It can only be condensed into one word: LOVE. This is the only thing we know.

After Terry became a Christian he had a strange responsibility to the woman he had been living with for six years. They had learned many things together—to be open and free with each other in conversation and in love. But she was a married woman; her husband was serving a term in prison.

After Terry accepted the Lord he didn't know what to do. Their little daughter was three years old. Six years together had meant a lot of sharing, a lot of inter-dependence. And he wondered, "Now what happens?" At first, he wanted her to get a divorce so they could be married and become a real family. He didn't want to be like his father and leave his child to be brought up without a daddy around.

During his six months at Mountaindale, Terry was praying; but he was afraid to go home because of the strength of the physical part of their relationship. He wrote only to his little daughter; and he asked the Lord,

"God, give me the grace to do what is right — what will be good for both of them and pleasing to You."

Then as he returned to the city he prayed,

"Lord, help me to see her as a soul — a child of yours, not just someone to go to bed with."

And when he finally went to see her one day, she came to him in a flood of emotion,

"Oh, Terry! I'm so happy to see you. I want you so. I need you. I've missed you terribly."

They had learned to be very frank with each other; they knew how to build each other up in love. And this made it even harder for Terry. She said again,

"Terry, I want you."

"I can't. I'm sorry."

"Why, Terry?"

"Because you're married . . . . "

"But I'm going to get a divorce."

"No, Phyllis, you can't."

"I am, Terry. I've waited and waited for you. I love you, Terry." And she started crying.

"Oh, God, help me," Terry cried out. And under his breath he prayed, "I can't. I can't. I can't. If I fall now, I'll never be able to help her find You, Lord, like I found You."

They knew each other as very warm, emotional, responsive persons; she was shocked at Terry's refusal. As he started to walk away, she reached out to him and looked into his face and whispered,

"Terry, do you want me to rape you?"

"Oh, Lord. No, Phyllis. Please understand," and he walked away, not looking back.

The next day she challenged him when he returned to take his daughter out.

"OK, Terry, tell her about this Jesus."

She couldn't understand what had happened to Terry, so he sat down and explained to her about Jesus Christ.

"Look, Phyllis, you're Jewish. You pray to God, don't you?"

"Yes . . . "

"All right. Let's pray to God then, and ask Him to reveal to you that Jesus Christ is His Son. You pray to Him every night and we'll see what happens."

First night, nothing. Second night she called him up.

"Terry, nothing's happened."

"Did you ask God?"

"Yes."

"Let's keep praying . . . "

The third night she called to say,

"Terry, I started praying the same way you told me to, and then I started to cry. And I saw a cross with many, many nails. And my hand reached out to take out the nails. And Terry, I believe. I believe. I believe."

"Thank you, God!"

This was the beginning of her direction. She started reading her Bible, and one day she said to Terry,

"I want to get a divorce, Terry, so we can be married and be a real Christian family—the three of us."

And Terry thought, "O Lord, what now?" He kept reading the nineteenth chapter of Matthew with her—the answers Jesus gave the Pharisees when they tested him with questions about divorce. But finally he had to leave New York. He knew he couldn't stay. It was too hard.

"Terry, don't leave us. What about your daughter? Live here and support her, at least."

"I can't. I can't stay. I'm going to Chicago, and start working on my education."

And he prayed, "Lord, You take away whatever might hinder me, whatever might be in my way. And he started crying because he didn't know what God was going to do. He didn't call home for two weeks, and when he did, she began to cry on the phone,

"Terry, I went to the prison and seen my husband. And, Terry, I love him. I still love him. What do I do now? I love you too."

"Look, dear lady, what God has put together let no man put asunder."

He knew this was the way it had to be. God had showed him, so he said without even hesitating,

"Stay with your husband."

"But how?"

"God knew all along that I was gonna get saved one day. Now He's saved you too; and your husband will get saved one of these days too."

"What about little Alicia?"

"God knows I have a daughter and He can take care of her too."

"But what about you, Terry? Are you all right? Are you happy?"

"I'm fine. Thank you for wanting to know, but I'll be just fine."

"Well, OK . . . " and there was a long silence. "What do we do now?"

"Pray."

So right there on the phone, between New York and Chicago, they prayed. God was in the finish, the mutual decision. If Terry had tried to figure it all out himself, it would have gotten all jumbled up. Now Terry preaches, works part-time, goes to school, and sends money home to help buy shoes and ice cream cones for his little daughter. He gave her a bicycle for Christmas; and when he dropped in to surprise her on her fifth birthday, she ran to him and said,

"Daddy, did you come all the way here just to see me?"

So much had changed in Terry's life. When the little girl was born, Terry was afraid to really love anyone. He was afraid to get that close until he let God come into his life.

22. Rudy

Rudy's father was a real Lothario—loved women, loved to drink; but he wanted to have it good for his family. The move he made from Puerto Rico to New York didn't work out as he had hoped, and he couldn't face seeing his family in such poor conditions. He felt so bad he drank some poison at his brother's place, then came home to die. Rudy was only six at the time.

Rudy and his older brother joined the same gang.

"We used to go out together," Rudy says. "Every guy that he used to fight with that was smaller, he would bring to me. When somebody bigger picked on me, I'd bring him in. My older brother, he was in the Seniors, and him and the head guys were always lookin' after us. Sometimes the Cubs would get in fights and some of the Seniors from a different gang would jump in and help us."

Rudy didn't finish school 'cause the gang fights got so tough. They were fighting against this rival gang, and this gang's territory was right where the school was. One day when they were fighting, they said they were gonna shoot one of Rudy's guys. So Rudy fired first and shot this guy in the leg. They all knew it was Rudy who done it. He got away, but they were all laying for him in school. He couldn't ever go back; he'd a got killed.

Rudy married when he was 17—a girl who lived in the next block. He was introduced to her at a party and they started talking and began to like each other.

Rudy was young and reckless. He got put away once in the Brooklyn Detention Home for having a .25 automatic. Somebody seen he was acting crazy-like and they got alarmed and called the cops. When they broke into his apartment the gun was there, so they took Rudy away. This was just life.

Rudy was feeling pretty sorry for himself sitting there in jail. His wife had separated from him and wouldn't even answer his letters. He didn't know what was happening with his little son. His mother was up tight, and his brother was strung out. And all of a sudden Rudy looked out and saw somebody walking by with a Bible.

"What's this?"

He knew this guy from the outside 'cause he used drugs too. When we'd go to jail, we'd see everybody from the neighborhood there—like a reunion. So they got to talking and this friend, Wayne, was telling Rudy all about Damascus Church and some camp he'd gone to and how he was "transformed."

Rudy didn't understand but when he left the jail he thought it would be a good idea to go to the church and see what was going on there. But he didn't do it. He tried to stay away from drugs, but he couldn't; and after a week back on junk he began to see himself right back in the same condition he was in before. He began to steal from his mother all over again, take everything from the house, break into cars and apartments, push guys off. And he was tired of this life; he knew exactly which way he was headed.

So what happened was he got to thinking about Wayne and this church he talked about in jail, and Rudy asked one of his friends if he would go with him to see what it was all about. Inside the church they seen guys they knew on the outside; guys that used to be stealing and shooting drugs in the basements of New York; guys that he never thought there was hope for. He'd known these fellows all his life, and just seeing them give Rudy more hope for himself. He made up his mind right away that if this was the answer, this was what he wanted.

He went upstairs and started talking to Mom Rosado about staying there in the church. She began talking about Christ and how wonderful He was, and she told him the experiences of this boy and that boy who were completely different now. It was the first time Rudy had seen addicts delivered from their habit any place!

Mom Rosado promised Rudy that if he would come back the next Thursday, she would have a place at the church for him to stay. Rudy's mother was so glad when he got home and told her what was going to happen and she gave him some money. That way he wouldn't have to steal and get busted and get put back in jail while he was waiting.

Rudy didn't want nothing to happen till Thursday, so he really had to scheme—angle here, hustle there. One day he saw this cap pistol; it cost him a dollar or something like that. Then he was talking to this "hick" who wanted to buy a gun and shoot somebody. Rudy's mind went into high gear, and he sold that little old cap pistol to the guy for $35! He probably saved somebody's life, you know; but that guy must have wanted to "ice" Rudy when he found out how he'd been took!

In the meantime Rudy told everybody in the neighborhood he was going to the church, and they was all hoping he'd make it clean. They wanted to see somebody they knew make it 'cause there'd be hope for them then too if they tried it. So Rudy didn't steal too much during that week; and he didn't go back to jail. And finally it was Thursday and he went to the church and filled in an application and they gave him a bed. Fellows were sleeping all over the place. Mom had a little parlor, and even her couch in there had somebody sleeping on it at nighttime.

One of the boys that went to the church with Rudy didn't want to make it; he wanted to go back out again. So Rudy told him,

"Don't fool with me. I been through all this. I'm tired of it. I lost my wife and I lost my son and I'm sick of going to jail. Stay away from me, man, with that stuff. I wanna change!"

So the friend went out and got high, and Rudy stayed for the service. He was already high when he came in that first night, but he went up to the altar at the end of the preaching anyway. He started nodding right there in front of the church on his knees; then he went into a daze, and finally went to sleep. Everybody thought he was really praying hard. Pee Wee went over and put his arms around him, and Rudy woke up and realized again where he was. And when Pee Wee asked him if he wanted to accept Christ as his Saviour from dope and everything, he said yes, not knowing what was going on.

The next morning when he woke up he felt uncomfortable. Physically his body was beginning to react; he didn't want to talk to nobody, or see nobody. He felt bad, even though he didn't have a very big habit then. He'd only been on the street a month and a week after he come out of jail, so he wasn't hooked too bad at that point. It took him five days, though, before he could really think about what had happened that first night. All the guys were talking to him about what God done for them, and they were praying for him.

It wasn't till later though, when Rudy went upstate to Mountaindale, that he began to understand what accepting Christ as his Saviour meant. Up there at the camp he had a chance and a place to pray, to read the Bible, to go to Bible study classes, to wake up in the morning with a heart full of thankfulness. There was nothing but addicts in Mountaindale, and here was a whole new life for them.

Rudy wasn't too happy to see Terry up there at camp, though. Terry had kidnapped Rudy in the Bronx; and he'd put a gun to his head one day when Rudy was dealing drugs, and took $45 off him. They used to really hate each other on the street. And what happens up at Mountaindale? They get in the same room like they was brothers!

One night up in Wisconsin after the drama was over Rudy was telling his story. Now you have to look a long way to find a man who looks any better than Rudy. God has really blessed him with a handsome appearance, but it's really a shock to see him after the drama. See, in the play he looks all filthy and raggedy and bloody, and when he "kicks cold turkey" he's a real animal. Then after the play's over, the boys all come out in their suits and ties to tell about they're being new creatures in Christ, and you hardly know they's the same men! There's Rudy looking like he stepped right out of a Fifth Avenue men's shop. He starts telling the audience about his wife and son—how he used to come home and little Rudy would run to him with his arms out, calling,

"Daddy, I haven't seen you for a long time!"

And Rudy said he would push him away. He wanted to pick him up and kiss him and hold him and laugh with him. He wanted to take him piggy-back to the park and play with him, but he couldn't. Rudy was an addict and he was bound up tight.

He went on to tell how he would lay in bed at night and cry,

"Please, God, why do I have to be like this?"

And in jail his mother would visit him and say,

"Rudy Boy, I hope you stay here. You're safe here. When you're in here I know you won't take an overdose and die."

And he explained how a man in prison tried to tell him there was hope, and how he turned his back like he didn't want to hear.

"I really wanted to throw my arms around him, and thank him," Rudy explained to the audience. "But it wasn't till later that I found for myself how good God is—how real Christ is!"

And the sadness and the joy of it all overwhelmed him so that the tears choked him and he couldn't finish his story.

That happens to all of us. We cry a lot. Rudy turned to the back of the platform and two of the fellows put their arms around him and stood there praying quietly with him while Jerry stepped in and thanked God for the miracle He had done in Rudy's life. One of the boys showing love to Rudy at the back of the platform was only five days old in the Lord! Man! It's beautiful what He can do!

But our problems aren't all just taken away like magic when we come to Christ. Rudy's wife sent him divorce papers, and she doesn't ever want to see him again. They were together about three years, and he put her through so much! Everytime he goes back to New York City he sees his little boy. He's a cute kid, and he's proud of his daddy. When Rudy picks him up, he feels it's just like they been together all the time. But he figures his wife may be better off free of him.

Rudy feels kind of like Paul did, that at this stage of his life it's better for him not to have anything to interfere with his ministry for the Lord. We're on the road a lot. Some days we get up at six o'clock in the morning, and don't go to bed until three. Some days we have almost entirely free; then we get together and open the Bible, and study, or discuss, or pray. We figure for God to use us, we must be refilled every day, every day. If a person comes needing help and we aren't filled with God, we aren't going to be able to help him.

God says, "I will give you back the years that the locust has eaten," and He is doing that in every way. Sometimes when all the guys are singing, I want to cry so bad—seeing all them guys singing and smiling, rejoicing in the Lord!

And we're praying for Rudy's brother—he's an addict too. Now a psychiatrist might tell you it's next to impossible for an ex-addict to live in the same room with an addict and not go back to using drugs. But Rudy went back to his mother's apartment in the Bronx to visit. It was small, so he and his brother had to share a room. One day Rudy went in there, and here was his brother taking off. The old feeling come over him, and his body screamed out for the stuff, but Rudy was saved! He couldn't understand how he could still have this deep-down desire for dope and be in the family of God.

He went all alone in the back room, and started praying,

"Lord, why should I go through this? I'm already saved, and I've got Your Holy Spirit living in me. I'm not supposed to have this craving; I'm supposed to be normal!"

For a half-hour Rudy begged God to deliver him from the desire. And He did. Now he goes home and he sees his brother using drugs right in front of him, and he immediately lets the Holy Spirit pray for him, in tongues he can't even understand. That's what He will do for us—in any tight spot. But we got to be willing to ask for His help and want it. We learn to let the Holy Spirit speak, and we listen to Him. This is the new experience that really keeps us going with Christ. It shows Christ so real to us, so practical in our lives.

Now Rudy was in Chicago. Him and Pee Wee's working with addicts who are so tired of drugs they want a way out. We make Faith Tabernacle our home in Chicago—north side, near Broadway and Irving Park. Lots of dope in the area. They been wonderful to us at the Tabernacle—let us put on the drama several times; they got room for us to sleep; they turn over the kitchen to us so we can feed the new guys as well as the old ones. They even give us the chance to study the Bible under some of God's great men—we really grew under the teaching of Dr. Derek Prince who was there a whole month. Let us use a room for our office.

Always something moving—most any time of day or night. People come in off the street for help—people praying, getting baptized with the Holy Spirit.

The guys work around the church—painting, construction, cleaning, taking part in the meetings. They take care of their own laundry, take turns in the kitchen, cooking and cleaning up. It's great! You can hear them singing, praising God, and God is there. The new guys know it too. They keep coming back—most of them—till they find out the secret for themselves.

23. Dannie

It was through the Narcotics Center in New York City that Dannie heard about Damasco. He'd gotten so tired of drugs, and he'd tried everything else. One day his psychiatrist told him, "I want to show you this letter." It was from one of the boys that Dannie knew, a fellow from the Bronx who'd been in and out of jail too,

"I'm having a great time up here in camp, and I thank God that you sent me here. God bless you!"

She went on reading, "God do this . . . and God do that . . . and you should see this place—it's beautiful."

All the time Dannie was standing there sick. When she got through reading the letter she looked at him and said,

"Would you like to go to this place?"

"A . . . to learn about God? I dunno."

Dannie had started his own gang in the Bronx. He was a good-looking, friendly, dark Negro. His dad worked for American Airlines, and he remembers his mother sitting by the window, talking to God about her nine kids. Dannie had lots of imagination. One day he was sitting on the stoop with some of the young guys in the neighborhood and he began to talk,

"You know, there was this guy and he runs with this real bad gang."

All the guys were lounging there, and they began to sit up and listen to Dannie. He always tells a good story anyway.

"Yeah, Dan. Go ahead. Tell us."

So Dan thought a minute and went on.

"His name was Baron. And he was a bad guy. Used to walk with a gun. Used to hit everybody—girls, 'n everybody! He was just real mean. Beat up this cop one time and went to jail, and . . . "

One of the guys jumped up and whispered, "Hey, man! Let's make a club!"

And Dannie said, "We can call ourselves the Barons! We'll be Barons all right!"

And somebody else added, "But we gotta get a reputation."

So they all got up off the stoop and headed for the junior high school. When they got there they went around slugging kids. About a dozen kids.

"But you know me," one little guy protested.

"Oh shut up! I'm a Baron."

It was weird. But it worked. From then on they could draft guys into their club, and they'd fall in because they knew the Barons had the reputation and nobody would mess with them. Most of the guys in the gang really did turn bad.

It was at a dance that somebody brought out the pack of marijuana.

"Hey! Try this reefer. This is what the older guys smoke."

Dannie and his friends were young punks—about 14, but they were already high from the liquor they drunk. So right away their senses were open to grab more.

It didn't look harmful. So they lit up and smoked it right on the street with people walking back and forth. Then they went back in the dance and sat down and Dannie told the guy,

"I don't feel anything."

He said, "Wait a while. You'll feel it."

And the next minute Dannie was under the table and they were dragging him outa the party. The cops came in and everything.

"This kid is too high on something. What did they give him?"

Everything in life seemed to happen like that you, you know? Big surprise!

Dannie got hooked on heroin through his gang too. One day he asked his buddy to buy him some reefers. Dan was working after school in a book bindery and he just got paid, so he gave his friend five dollars. When this kid came back he handed Dan a little white bag.

Dan looked at the little bag and he's thinking of all the reefers he could smoke and all the whiskey he could drink, so he was mad.

"This bag ain't gonna do nothin' to me! Gimme my money back, or we gonna fight! Just this little tiny bag for five dollars?"

"Man! You know what this'll do? It'll get you high, and you high, and you high, and the other guy over there high."

They went back to the club and got the rest of the guys, and they all went to the bathroom. Dan was really angry because he'd spent $5 on that little bag and he was sure it wasn't gonna do a thing.

"If it don't, we're gonna take him over and . . . "

"I'm tellin' ya, boy," this kid kept on. "This is gonna get you high!"

Dan took about four sniffs of this powder in his nose, and the kid told him,

"No more! The rest of the guys gotta get some."

They passed it around and pretty soon Dan looked at this kid. He was high all right. He was like going to sleep. This was something. He would scratch his nose. His mouth was turned down. But Dannie said,

"I don't feel nothing! C'mon gang, le's beat up this guy."

See, the first time you do it, you have your mind set that it won't do anything so it won't make an effect on ya too bad. Like blotting it out.

"You still got it in your nose, Dannie. It's not in you yet."

"What're ya' talking about?"

"Look, Baby. Put one finger here, and just breathe up real hard."

Dan done that on one side of his nose, and he done it on the other side, and before he knows it, he was just like his buddy was. They walked down to the Community Center and Dan was high all right. People were looking at him, but they weren't sure. They seen addicts before, but he was young. The older guys, they threw him out, but they weren't sure either. They never seen kids high so young. The Barons were in junior high school. This is what the East Side got plagued with—young kids using drugs. We knew a lot of kids who were snorting.

Anyway, Dan was way out, like throwing up his guts and everything and saying, "Boy! this is great!" And he was hurting inside. And saying, "Wow! I'm gonna do this everyday!"

This is the way heroin makes you feel. You're completely out of it. Closed off. In a different world.

He still felt the effects of the drug the next day — like weak and dizzy. He was still high; it was still going through his system. Somebody told him,

"Drink some cold water, and the feeling will come up more."

He did and he felt a little more. And when he got paid again he said to the same boy,

"Let's buy some more and try and shoot it. They say you get higher than sniffing it. Let's see what happens."

So they walk up to the dealer, "Look, gimme a bag."

And the pusher looks down and says, "Get outa here, Shorty, I don't give drugs to kids. What are ya, crazy?

They asked another fellow who was an addict, and he bought the stuff for them. Before he stuck the needle in he pinched Dan's arm so he wouldn't feel it. Then he shot the stuff in.

Dan's heart started beating fast, and the guy looked at him and said,

"How do ya feel? Wait a minute. Wait a minute. What're ya doin'?"

'Aw, I don't feel nothin'." Dan was feeling plenty but he was scared.

They could see he was gagging, and couldn't breathe. He was like going out.

"If you feel a rush like you might explode, like the blood is shooting to your head, it's the drugs. You gotta move, man! If you stay still you'll catch an overdose and die. You have to make it go round your system—get it outa your heart. You shoot the drug and it stays together in one place. Your heart starts beating real fast, and before you know it you lose your wind. You gotta move or you'll die, kid."

Dannie made it with drugs for six years but his own brother and sister did catch an overdose and die.

The drug addict has a tremendous mind and a tremendous need. Dan had all these different personalities he would use on people — to get dope, to get money, to make it into a hospital, to find a way. He learned to read people like they was books. He'd get a first impression of a person and then he'd speak to him. If he seemed sorry for him, then he'd use that approach; if he didn't, he'd act superior. "If you have to lower yourself, you'll do that," said Dan. You learn a great thing in "conning."

Even the social workers you try to con. Dannie was great at this. He used to pop up out of nowhere. This man, Bob, with the Education Alliance, would go someplace to a nice restaurant to eat, and there would be Dan — a drug addict, standing at his elbow. He would hear Dan tell him how he needed money for something and Bob would say,

"I can't give you money, Dannie, but I can treat you. Come on and eat with me."

"But I don't want anything to eat. Gimme the money."

"I'm sorry, I can't. Eat."

He didn't want to feel guilty about getting Dan further involved. Bob even invited Dan to live in his house, and Dan did for awhile; but a junkie can't help himself. Dan didn't mean to take his friend's radio; he didn't want to hurt Bob. One day he said,

"It's all your fault, you know. You got involved with me. I didn't come into your life; you came into mine. You said you could help me."

This really broke Bob up. Like man! He really dug Dannie.

A lot of people find it easy to like Dan. And that day at the Narcotics Center the psychiatrist tried again to reach him. As he walked out of the room she called after him, "When you really get up tight, it's time to pray, Dan."

That same day Dan lost his job as a brick layer. He was so weak he could hardly lift a brick. And worse yet, he just wasn't thinking about bricks; he was only thinking about dope all the time.

He got paid, and spent all the money on drugs. He gave all his friends fixes. Whenever Dan had money, he'd say to somebody nearby, "Come on. I get you high." He didn't want to be alone—you give dope to other people just to make sure there's someone with you.

The next day he woke up sweating and sick and he just lay there looking around the room. He was a Catholic, and he prayed, "Oh God. Help me!" Then he got dressed and went down to the Narcotics Center, and they told him he could leave for this church in a couple hours. He went back to the place where he been staying with a buddy, and stole everything there and sold it for dope. He wanted to be sure he would feel all right for whatever it was that was going to happen.

When they got to Damascus Church Dan looked around,

"Wow! This is nothing. Cracks in the walls."

He seen guys mopping the floor, praising the Lord. He seen guys downstairs cooking, singing "Bless this food." Everybody was saying, "God bless you, brother!" Everybody putting me on, he thought. He was looking around at everything, and Pop Rosado told us, "Watch this guy. He's going to give us a lot of trouble."

When we got ready to eat, we told Dan, "Just a minute. We're gonna say grace."

"OK, go ahead. I'm gonna eat."

"We'd like you to stand up with us."

"Aw, gee whiz! All right," and he looked around at everybody with their heads bowed.

After we ate, the guys were walking around singing "Praise the Lord." Guys were upstairs in the temple praying; they come to Dannie to pray for him, but Dannie said,

"No. You don't have to pray for me. It's all right, y'know. I just wanna look around."

Then Lennie came in from Mountaindale. He's an exciting person; he has an interesting face. That's what partly attracts you. He came up to Dan, "God bless you!"

And Dan looks at this guy, and his face lights up: Wow! And right away Lennie's preaching. This young guy just walks in and he's speaking about God, but also he's speaking Dannie's language, "Christ can do it, man. Dig it!"

Ron's sitting there with this big hole in his T-shirt, and he's listening to every word as Lennie tells him his experiences with God,

"I was in the camp, and I was praying and I felt the presence of

God. You know, Solomon felt the presence of God." And he went on to speak about people in the Bible like he knew them.

All this time Dan was leaning over close to hear. When Lennie saw how interested he was he took Dan's hand and said, "God bless you" again.

Dan didn't want to let go; he answered:

"God bless you, too. And tell me some more about — you know, God."

Later on in the service, one of the boys was preaching in Spanish. Dan was sitting there looking as hard as a bag of nails again—real mean. He had his arms stretched out on the back of the pew, like he was thinking, "Go ahead. I don't care."

Then all of a sudden he snapped to attention and he was thinking, "Suppose there is a God? Suppose there is a Christ that died? Suppose I am a sinner like these guys say — that I need salvation. You tried hospitals, Stupid. You tried everything else. Nobody wants you; go to God."

Then he got this vision of Christ standing there, so hazy he could hardly make Him out. He was crying but he didn't even know it. The guy next to him nudged him and said,

"What're ya crying about?"

"I don't know!"

The service lasted four hours, and on the way out of the temple somebody said to Dan, "God is calling you." This really threw him. They showed him his bed—but he couldn't sleep because of his habit. He was tossing and turning; and he didn't know what it was, but he heard a voice telling him,

"Go upstairs and pray."

And all the time the thought was going through his head: "God is calling you, like this guy said." But he put the covers over his head. He couldn't tell where the voice was coming from. He was laying there thinking, "Should I go upstairs or what?" Then all of a sudden he just froze. It was like the Lord came to him and talked to him. Dan sat up and listened, and he heard the voice again.

That time he got up and went upstairs. As soon as he got in the temple he felt this weight, a tremendous weight dragging on him. Each time he'd take a step down the aisle he'd stop by one of the pews and say, "God! Have mercy." By the time he got to the altar at the front he was drenched in tears, "God, forgive me! Have mercy. Have mercy." He just wept and wept.

"I didn't know You was real. I didn't know You was real. I didn't know You was real."

24. Jerry

Jerry was five when his father deserted his mother. She had to go to work so she put Jerry in an orphanage. And from there he went to another orphanage. One day a man came to see him — a big, husky man. It was Jerry's dad.

"I never seen him before," Jerry says. "My mother told me he was dead. I had no feeling. I didn't love him and I didn't hate him. There was just indifference, coldness. He had bummed his way around the country and then joined the Army. Somewhere along the way he met God and he wanted to make up all those lost years to us. I used to see him once or twice a year after that, but I just didn't care."

Jerry left the orphanage when he was fifteen, and went to live in a foster home in Brooklyn. The next year he quit school and lived with his dad in Florida and Ohio a few months. His dad introduced him to Christian people and kept telling about Christ all the time. But he didn't pay no mind to what his father said. It just meant nothing.

While he was in Toledo with his father, Jerry joined the Air Force—but he only stayed with that four months. Then he went back to New York to live with his mother. Started hanging around with the gang and started smoking marijuana. The cats in his gang told him to try it and he figured they looked all right.

"In fact," he told me, "they looked happier than I was, and I wasn't sad."

Pot gave Jerry a new kind of freedom. He was lonely now, and smoking pot made him feel good; he could speak to people easier. Not that he couldn't talk before, but with pot he just felt freer. Then he started sniffing heroin. Then skin popping in the muscle. Then he took a mainliner—all pretty close together. That was it. His life really changed. He thought he had found something nobody else had.

A shot of dope. A good feeling. His senses were really keyed up. Jerry enjoyed music. The guys and gals would congregate in a pad, some smoking reefers, others shooting dope. And there would always be music—progressive jazz—Bud Shank, Charley Parker, J. J. Johnson, Stan Getz.

Jerry's mother couldn't understand him even before he got hooked. She was from Russia. Her ways were old country ways; and Jerry didn't try much to understand her. They had no real relationship, just lived in the same apartment.

One morning when Jerry got out of bed, he said to his mother,

"Look, Ma. I gotta have $5 for a shot of dope. I don't care where you get it, but get it."

By this time Jerry was skinny; he had holes in his shoes. His mother looked at him and said,

"Jerry, you know I'm on welfare. I get relief checks, and you take my checks and forge them and spend the money on dope. You take my money for rent and for food and you spend it on dope. Everything you get your hands on you take to the pawn shop to get money for dope."

As she was speaking to him Jerry had his hands on her shoulders and was edging her out the open window behind her. She begged and pleaded with him,

"Please, Jerry. Be careful, son."

"Look, Ma, I gotta have $5, and I gotta have it now."

He looked at her as if she was a piece of wood, a sheet of glass or metal.

"What do I care about you?" And he was gonna let her go out the window. But something kept him, and he turned her around and shoved her out the door instead.

"Look, Ma. You get out and get me $5. I don't care where you get it, but get it!"

"Jerry, please. The neighbors will know why I'm borrowing money."

But the door was locked and she was out in the hall. Her only child, her only son wouldn't let her into her own house. She came back with four dollars, but he wouldn't open the door.

"No, Ma. Four dollars is not enough. Can't you understand? The pusher's not gonna take four. He wants five. I gotta have $5, Ma. Four won't do."

Deep inside himself Jerry wanted to reach out and open the door. He wanted to pull her inside and hold her quietly and tell her, "Ma, I'm sorry. I can't help myself. I don't want to do what I'm doing. I don't mean to say the things that I'm saying. I don't want to treat you like this. I can't help myself, Ma. Dope comes first in my life. You're nothing. I gotta have my dope. Please, Ma. Help me."

When you look at people all you see is their money. While you still got the needle in your arm, you're thinking about the next shot: how am I gonna get $5 again? You don't care about anybody else except yourself. Maybe they don't have food. Maybe they're poor. Maybe they have little children. But you just don't care. One of the guys took a baby out of a baby carriage. He laid the baby on the ground and took the carriage and sold it for dope.

Jerry'd been on drugs about a year when he was busted for possession of works. Since it was the first time, he got probation, and went up to a resort in Spring Valley to work.

That's when he met the girl. She was taking care of an old man there at the resort. Pretty soon they moved in together. Then Jerry broke his probation when they left Spring Valley and started traveling across the country. She knew he was a drug addict—she was not. She was married and had three children, but she left it all to be with Jerry.

Actually he couldn't tolerate her unless he was high; only then would he do anything to please her. Even when he couldn't stand her though, he wanted her around, somebody to speak to, to be with. She was a smart girl, but she would do anything for Jerry. She did do anything for him — stole, cheated, sold her body, bore his children, put up with his abuse and rejection for four years. I believe she really loved him.

She'd never lived this kind of life before. He was stealing from department stores; and he'd get her to bring the merchandise back for a refund. It was weird. But he had to have money, 'cause he had to have the dope. When he couldn't get heroin he'd take seconals, terpin hydrate, paregoric, benzedrine, dexedrine, nembutals. The girl would get them for him in the drug store. Sometimes he'd look so bad the pharmacist wouldn't sell him anything. He took all sorts of things—stimulants and depressants—together, trying to find a happy medium. Goofballs would get him very sleepy; then he'd swallow a few benzedrine with some hot tea to make them work very quickly. His eyes would get like half dollars. He couldn't stop talking, couldn't stop smoking. His movements were jerky. He'd find it was too much, so he'd take a few more goofballs to bring him down a little. Life was just back and forth.

Jerry and the girl had three children. She didn't care much for the kids; she just cared for being with Jerry—said she couldn't live without him. They kept the babies with them for a while, but they got in the way. Jerry had to go into Chicago from Ft. Wayne or Indianapolis on weekends to get his dope. The first baby they took along with them; then another one came, and it got to be too much of a chore, so they put them in different adoptive homes.

Jerry was working for an encyclopedia company, selling door-to-door. He'd work when he felt like it—get high and be inspired and go knock on a door. Sometimes he'd even make a sale. He was on commission. One of the fellows there at the company sold them his car, but they took off and never paid him. They had an income tax refund check that came back just in time for them to head west, so they went clear out to Las Vegas. There Jerry stole and the girl sold her body for him—to get dope. Jerry knew he was hurting this girl; it was just because of him she was doing these things. They made enough to travel and buy dope. And they finally ended up in San Francisco.

That's where Jerry would go to Macy's, to Broadway's and Sears—to steal pants. He'd go into the fitting room and put on two pairs under his own and walk out. The girl was pregnant, so she couldn't go out in the streets and hustle for him. Pretty soon he used up all the stores in San Francisco, and he had to go down to Los Angeles. It was down there he got arrested trying to steal more pants. When the officer looked at his arms and saw Jerry was an addict, he dropped the theft charge and charged him with internal possession. If you have fresh marks on your arm, this is enough for an arrest in California.

The girl came down twice from San Francisco to visit him in jail, but after that she never showed up again. When Jerry came out of the prison, he had two dollars and he didn't know what to do or where to go. The girl was like a big crutch for him, but he had lost her. He called up his dad in Miami to see if he would help him, and they told him he was dead. He got a job for several months working for an ambulance company in Los Angeles until he had enough money to get back to New York. For some reason he didn't have the heart to steal no more.

In New York heroin was hard to get so Jerry was gulping more and more pills. He got a drug store connection, a pharmacist who would give him pills behind the counter.

Then a cousin, who was a psychiatrist, took an interest in him and got him into a private mental hospital. He went through every kind of therapy except shock treatment—psycho therapy, group therapy, creative therapy, occupational therapy, tranquilizers. But after nine months there he was only worse. It was about this time that he really began to believe this thing about being a confirmed addict. He thought, "This is my life. This is all of it. There is nothing for me except dope."

Three times a week, forty-five minutes each time, a psychiatrist there in the hospital would ask Jerry about his life—probing, searching. He was not accustomed to working with addicts; and he was pretty nervous himself—like he'd smoke two packs of cigarettes during the session. Jerry thought he was a real nice guy; they smoked the same brand.

Then Jerry registered for occupational therapy, but he soon found out he was very bad at knocking out copper ashtrays and making wallets. Some people can do that all day; it seems to occupy their empty spaces. But for Jerry it was just too much; the whole thing bored him.

In creative therapy they explain to you about the difference between integration and disintegration. Then they give you paints and colors and paper and tell you, "Now integrate!" Jerry said, "I can't paint." He tried with the rest of the patients, but it was no good.

Five or six patients met regularly with two psychiatrists for group therapy. Everybody spoke about life as they knew it, their own personal feelings. Usually it was just a conversation, something to enjoy; you got a laugh out of it once in a while. It was a lot better than knocking out ashtrays! But it wasn't enough.

After Jerry left, he went of his own volition to one state hospital; then he got out of there and went into another one, under the pretense of being loaded on pills and having bad dreams. They won't even let you fill out an application if they know you're an addict. After he got into the hospital he said,

"Look, I'm a drug addict. I need something."

"Why didn't you tell us when you came in?"

"I didn't think you'd accept me if you knew."

They kept him and he was safe for about eight weeks. Sometimes there's no other place to turn. It's a haven where you have somebody to depend on. You don't have to make any decisions yourself. On weekends Jerry would go home and get high. Still it was a refuge to protect him from himself, and it gave his mother a chance to breathe. Then he was out again and he caught a series of overdoses. He was standing in front of his house, and the next thing he knew they were wheeling him into an ambulance. Or he was in the bathtub, and his mother ran hysterical to the neighbors for help, "My son! My son is dying!" Another time he was eating scrambled eggs at the kitchen table with his mother, and he fell on the floor. Two guys were picking him up when he regained consciousness.

There was no way out for Jerry. He took six OD's at various times. Once he found himself on the subway tracks. It was late at night. He'd just gotten his dope Downtown and he was standing on the platform waiting for a train. The next things he knew he was laying on the tracks. His head was split open, blood was gushing down his face. And right behind him was the third rail — another couple inches and he would have been electrocuted. There were only a few people on the platform. He didn't know whether a train was coming or not. He didn't really want to die, yet he didn't care. He was in a semi-conscious overdose state—not completely out, when two fellows jumped down and picked him up. The cops came with an ambulance and took him over to Fordham Hospital.

Jerry woke up in a cubicle with padded walls. He didn't know where he was or how long he'd been there. It could have been four years that he laid on the tracks. Nothing made any difference. Life was just a big round zero—a blank.

When you're an addict the days pass, then the weeks, the months. The years go by and nothing has happened. All you got to show for living is marks on your arm. After while you're hardly even getting high. You just need a shot to get low, so you're able to function. You become a reject. You don't care for nothing. You cry in the darkness and loneliness of the night. In the brightness of noon there's only night. You're always alone. Even Jerry's cousin, the psychiatrist, gave up after awhile; he didn't want to have anything more to do with Jerry. Jerry didn't believe in nothing or nobody. The doctors all said, "I doubt if he'll ever make it." He had resigned himself to a life of dope addiction.

Then one day in the grocery store a man told Jerry that strange things were happening to addicts at Damascus Church. Now he didn't care much about going to a church—even the name of Jesus Christ was offensive to him, a Jew. But the grocer started telling him about this camp, where the addicts were going, and Jerry thought that would be all right. Certainly a camp would be better than a mental hospital. He had a hammer in his hand, looking to break into a car and he decided to walk into the church just out of curiosity.

Right away he seen and heard these fellows praising God—seen the shine on their faces, like a radiance there. He knew a couple of them — shot dope with them, got high with them. And he couldn't believe it! And like the rest of us Jerry thought to himself, "What's the gimmick?" Then like they knew what he was thinking, a couple of these guys came over and said, "You don't have to shoot dope any more. Jesus is the answer."

Jerry seen a spark of life, but he couldn't understand it. He figured they was getting high on something different. Whatever it was he wanted it. So he began asking,

"God, if you're real, do something for me too."

There were only a few who were Jewish out of all the guys I knew at Damasco. It's unusual for a Jewish boy to walk into a church. He has to be in terrible shape — like Jerry. He had a pair of pants on that were so crusted at the knee — filthy! He had holes in his shoes. He was dirty, skinny, kicking a habit. And not a pill left in his pocket.

But Jerry went up to the chapel to pray, and something came over him — a feeling like he was being washed. All that garbage and corruption was being cleaned out of Jerry, and he didn't know what was happening to him. But the next day when he walked out on the street he felt alive. He began to walk like somebody had removed a weight from his legs. He could see like somebody had taken a blindfold off his eyes. Everything was new: the children, the buses, the subways, the traffic. And tears of joy started rolling down his face.

"Everytime I started to cry," Jerry says, "it was like all the grief and all the misery was pouring out of me. All the heartache and the suffering and the anguish. All the thirteen years of drug addiction, the loneliness. And I knew I was no longer alone. I knew that Jesus Christ was real, and that he was performing in my life, my heart, something new."

25. Louis

Louis was born in Puerto Rico and when he was four his father left the island to go to New York. It was six years before he sent for his family to join him. They didn't know nothing about America—couldn't speak English. But they went, and two days after they got to New York, Louis' father went away and never came back.

Louis and his sister and mother waited in the apartment, but the father had deserted, as so many do. The mother had to go out to find some kind of a job. There was no one to turn to. She left the children alone in the Simpson Street apartment. One day she came home from her job as a sewing machine operator to find the whole inside of the house burned out — no clothes left or nothing. The kids had been playing with matches.

The first Christmas in New York, Louis insisted they keep the Puerto Rican custom of cutting grass and making little nests in the house for Santa Claus.

"I remember that Christmas Eve," Louis told me. "We put the grass and the note to Santa under the bed. Me and my sister were making a big noise—we were so happy. But my mother just sat down and looked at us. Pretty soon she started crying and we didn't know what was wrong with her. When I asked her, 'What's wrong with you, Mums?' she didn't say nothing."

The children went to bed early so they could get up early. But when they got up, their mother was still sitting in the same chair.

"You been sitting there all night, Mums?" Louis asked her, and she said she couldn't sleep. When they ran to find what was in the grass, there was nothing. Louis turned to his Mom,

"Where's the toys that Santa brought us?"

And for the first time in his life he listened to her tell them that Santa Claus was not real — that she was Santa Claus, and that this year she couldn't get them nothing 'cause she didn't have no money.

Louis cried as he stumbled downstairs looking at the other kids in the building with their new toys. Out on the street he looked in the store windows till he came to one where he seen a beautiful doll. He went inside, and when nobody was looking, he grabbed the doll and took it home for his sister.

Louis was 10 years old then. It was the first time in his life he had ever taken anything that didn't belong to him. But from then on he took everything he could get his hands on.

Three years later Louis started smoking pot. There was so much sadness, so little hope in his life after he came to America and his father ran away and left the family. His mind was open; he was always looking for a new experience that would give him more joy. In school he wanted to be popular. He started hanging out with the wrong crowd. He began smoking, then drinking, going to dances; and somewhere along the way somebody gave him a "stick." Marijuana was good. It was pleasure. It gave him courage. He just went for this new kick. Then one day he was introduced to heroin. He knew it wasn't good for him — he'd seen drug addicts. But he was thinking that he had the will power. Two weeks later he discovered that drugs had become part of his life, part of his body, part of his blood. In two weeks!

In order to survive then he had to learn how to use and hurt people. And Louis never wanted to hurt people. He took everything away from the house—the only thing his mother had left was a little bit of life, and he almost took that away from her.

There was this one morning Louis got up at home. He was sick, and he asked himself, "Where are you going today? Where will you get money? You're broke. You haven't got any place to go for money. You know you're gonna be sicker and sicker."

He went downstairs and started working and working, just trying to see if he could make it. His body's hurting, he's sweating. Then he seen this man coming by. He looked clean, and Louis thought, "Maybe that man would give me two dollars." So he took a chance. He told him straight,

"I need two dollars for a bag of drugs. If you don't give it to me, I'm gonna hurt you."

The man said, "If you want two dollars you're gonna have to kill me."

So they started fighting. Louis had a razor in his hand and he cut the man, his back and his throat. And he went into his pocket and there was two dollars, the only money the man had. Louis took the money and ran off and got high. Then he came back home and went to sleep. The police arrived and arrested him and took him to the Brooklyn Detention House. There he waited, thinking about his future—a lifetime behind bars. Eventually they gave him one day to life. He could have stayed his whole life behind bars. Ten years, fifty, forever. But after thirty-six months in jail he came out on a discharge.

The day before he came out—he was supposed to go home the next morning, he started getting nervous. After three years behind bars he was going to be free to go home, to start a new life! But he began asking himself, "Now that I'm going home what am I gonna do? Now that I'm gonna be free, am I going back to drugs? Am I going back home to hurt my mother all over again?"

And he started smoking cigarette after cigarette. He's scared. He seen himself ragged, dirty, skinny. He knew what's out there. He knew what he's going to face as soon as he walked out the door. He knew the drugs that were waiting for him, and he knew he'd be tempted to use them. He wanted to change his life. He wanted to start all new. He wanted to please his mother, to help her. He wanted to get a job, and maybe marry a beautiful woman.

Finally he heard, "OK, Louis. Come on out. Bring your stuff."

He was so nervous he could hardly walk. He almost fell down three times, he was so scared. As the bus got closer to New York City he was asking himself: What am I gonna do first?

At the terminal he took the subway north. And as he got off the train in the Bronx he started seeing police, the same police that had slapped him so many times. He seen the same guys he shot dope with, stole with. He seen boys high, goofing on the corners and on the stoops. He seen the police chasing somebody on the rooftops, and somebody running down the fire escape. The same old neighborhood, the same old mess, and he's getting sick. He asked himself, "Should I take a shot, or shouldn't I take a shot? Maybe if I just take one shot, I can stop." So he took a chance. He went and got a shot—even before he got home. They gave him $20 when he got out of prison so the money was right in his pocket.

Meanwhile, back home his mother was waiting for Louis. She came to the door and kissed him. Then she held him back and looked at him, and she knew.

"Louis, what are you trying to do? Are you trying to take my life away — to kill me? I've taken you to hospitals. I've taken you to Puerto Rico. I've taken you every place I know. I've done everything I know how to do. And after thirty-six months of being clean, you come back, and right away you're doing the same thing. God help you, Louis. I'm washing my hands of you from today on."

Louis' mother had sacrificed her life for him. She never made any complaints, even though he hurt her a lot. She tried so hard for so long. Now she was through. There were tears in her eyes. Louis was hurt bad too, and she knew it. But there was nothing more she could do. Louis was dead to her from that day on.

He came downstairs, crying and running at the same time, and he bumped into a guy he knew. He was an addict just like Louis. But something was different — he wasn't filthy and raggedy, and he said,

"God bless you, Louis!"

It was Lennie that bumped into Louis that day. This cat was all dressed up in a white shirt and tie, and Louis knew he was an addict just like him. But his hair was cut, and he had a Bible under his arm, and he stopped to say,

"God bless you, Louis! Look at me. Jesus changed my whole life! I don't have to shoot drugs no more. I found the way out, Louis; I'm in church now. I know the church can help you too."

Louis brushed past him and kept going. All he could think was, "Without my mother I won't be able to do nothing. I got no place to eat, no place but the rooftops to go to."

Lennie called after him,

"I'm praying for you, Louis, and I'll be waiting for you!"

But Louis was rejecting him,

"Don't tell me nothin' about God, 'cause I don't wanna know about God." And he kept running on down the steps and out the door, still crying.

Louis went his own way and soon was hooked again. Only now as he looked at the needle and the blood going up and down, different thoughts went through his head, "What about this boy that used to be just like me? What is this Jesus he said changed his life? Could this Jesus really help me?" And everytime Lennie saw Louis he told him he was still praying for him.

During that year Louis' mother gave him another chance and let him come back home to live. But one day he stole a typewriter from the house and she called the police and they arrested him.

This time he was so disgusted with himself that he went straight from the prison to the church when he was let out. It was raining, and he was already high, walking along talking to himself, "When am I going to stop? Why do I have to shoot drugs? Why do I have to hurt my mother? Why do I have to suffer like this? Why do I have to go to jail?"

As he walked in the rain a lady bumped into him and said, "God bless you." Louis stopped right in the middle of the sidewalk and just stared at her. She gave him a piece of paper and he stood there with people rushing past him, reading and remembering what Lennie had told him. He stuffed that paper in his pocket and headed for the church to look for Lennie.

When he came in somebody told him Lennie was upstairs with the drug addicts. Louis walked up the stairs and he saw all these boys who had been like him, only now they're happy. Lennie came over as soon as he saw Louis, and said, "Come on, Louis," and he introduced him to all these boys who had been on drugs many years. Then he put his arm around Louis' shoulders and said, "Louis, we're gonna pray for you."

All of the guys went into the temple, and Louis got down on his knees with them and they started to pray. He listened to Lennie asking God to help him, to change his life, and he started to weep. He was weeping and weeping and weeping like he never wept before in his whole life. And he cried out to God,

"Please, God. Have mercy on me. I'm sick. I'm tired of life. I don't even wanna live no more. If You changed Lennie's life, please change mine too."

Even when he got off his knees Louis felt different. He said,

"I'm not just sure what's happening, but I feel like I got something to look forward to. My whole mind is different. I want to serve God."

26. Tony

Tony was one of the few guys in the Bronx that got all the way through high school before he got hooked. His family wasn't rich but they all had a good education, and as a child living in Puerto Rico he had everything he needed. His mother and father were divorced when he was very small, about two years old. After his mother left the Caribbean for New York, Tony lived with his aunts—one a secretary for a doctor, one a teacher. His father was a barber.

"I used to see my father every day," Tony says, "but I never lived with him. I set up my values with my grandmother and my aunts. I belonged more with them. They said I looked like my father and I was very fond of him."

Tony was 13 when he left San Juan and came to New York City with his aunts. From the time he was a very young boy Tony liked joking around. And he liked girls very much too, and night life.

"You be a good boy, Tony, and you'll have whatever you want," his aunts told him.

He had a lot of clothes and plenty of money. He had graduated from junior high and was doing well at Central Commercial High School, 42nd Street and Third Avenue. So he figured,

"This is great! I be a good boy. I have a lot of fun. I don't do anything against the law. This is life."

Then one day he began using pot.

Tony lived near Columbia University and many of the students there were smoking marijuana. This is something common. It just shows up more in the slums because you have to do too many things that aren't legal in order to buy narcotics; then it comes to the light of the law. If you have money to buy it when you want it, it doesn't become such an issue.

Right now there's an association of college students in Greenwich Village called LEMA—Legalized Marijuana. There's nothing big in it, they say. It's not habit forming, physically speaking. But mentally you can get hooked.

Charles Beaudelaire, the French writer, in "The Poem of Hashish" says that the supreme thought bursting from the user's dream is, "I have become God."

But he goes on to tell about the terrible tomorrow:

"All the body's organs lax and weary, nerves unstrung, itching desires to weep, the impossibility of applying oneself steadily to any task—all these cruelly teach you that you have played a forbidden game . . . the special victim is the will . . . it is the nature of hashish (or marijuana) to weaken the will."

Even if it does give you the ability to go deeper into music and poetry and love and everything, it takes away your ability to use the increased awareness. Beaudelaire also said,

"He who has recourse to poison in order to think will soon be unable to think without poison."

But Tony kept on smoking pot and he graduated from high school and was ready to enter City College. About the same time he realized he wanted money to keep up the good life he was living, so he went to work with Columbia Pictures as an IBM operator instead. He made good money, had good clothes and a few girls he could count on. They used to go to night clubs every weekend.

"I had me a ball," Tony said, "and I thought this was the life." I was still doing things that were accepted by society—with the exception of marijuana. But this was such a little thing; I thought it was not important."

What he didn't count on was the day coming when marijuana wouldn't do too much for him anymore. He got up to maybe seven reefers at a time to get high, while before he only needed one. Marijuana was letting him down, and besides it was getting pretty expensive. He had to spend sometimes even ten dollars every two days. His happiness was fading and he wondered what next.

He used to go nightclubbing every weekend with an old high school friend. One night his friend introduced Tony to heroin; he was just a beginner himself.

Right there in the nightclub Tony snuffed his first heroin up his nose, and he didn't like it. It made him feel real sick and throw up. But he also felt kind of a nice sensation inside. It's true that dope does something to you both physically and mentally. It makes you feel relaxed. So the next day Tony called up the same boy,

"Why don't we try it again? I got money."

Tony seen what heroin could do to people, but this was the way his heart fooled him—in just the mere thought:

"I'm a smart boy and I'm not going to destroy my life; I know what's happening."

This time he went to a skin pop into the muscle. Now he's still smart. He knows he's gotta work Monday. So he's not gonna touch it Monday, Tuesday, Wednesday, Thursday. Only on the weekend . . .

And that's what he did for nine months—heroin just on weekends. He was clean. He had a lot of suits. He had a few girls. Man! This wasn't too bad. He figured if he could hang on like this for nine months he could do it all his life. Tony was pretty smart!

Then one morning he woke up — his nose was running; he had pains all over his legs; his bones hurt; and then he began throwing up. And Tony says, "What is this?" He ran out of the house and bought a bag of dope, and injected the stuff into his vein. Everything was fine again. He was completely relaxed. And he was hooked!

Yeah, Tony was a smart boy! He was the only one of our group who was smart enough to get all the way through high school before he got hooked. But I guess all the education in the world can't keep you from getting hooked, if you got that big emptiness inside you and you start filling it up with junk.

Then it came Mondays and Wednesdays and Saturdays—the sickness. And as the habit grew, the expense grew. It was only a few weeks until he was spending $10 a day to cure his body. He would take a bag in the morning; and then at night he was so sick he needed another bag to go to sleep. Seventy dollars a week on junk left him only $20 for everything else, so he began borrowing money — from the groceryman, laundryman, the people where he worked. And he used to pay them back on the weekend when he got paid.

The habit grew to $15 every day, and he couldn't pay nobody anymore. So he began pawning things—graduation ring, watch; and he owed so many people money he had to escape from them all the time. Instead of coming up this block he'd have to go up the other block so they'd not see him. Then he had to quit his job. They found out he was sleeping on the machines, nodding at his work. And he looked different: he was growing thinner; he didn't get a haircut no more; his eyes were glassy; he was degrading himself in every way. They let him know that they knew something was wrong. He tried to tell them he was planning on getting married and that his girl left him. They were going to give him a break; and then they found out he was a drug addict.

His aunts that he was living with found out too. He hadn't touched any of their property; didn't like to steal. He thought he could use other methods to get money. He sold all his suits, lost his girl friends, went to Metropolitan Hospital, got busted by the police, kicked his habit cold turkey in the prison. Then his mother and his aunts cleaned him up, bought him new suits, gave him money to go to Puerto Rico, and Tony started all over again.

His father had a large graduation picture of Tony hanging in his barber shop in San Juan. He was proud that Tony was coming back to visit him after seven years in America. He hugged and kissed him and introduced him happily to all his friends. He had told them all what a wonderful son he had. And in three weeks, Tony looked like a bum. He began stealing from the barber shop, from his grandmother's home, and from other Puerto Rican houses.

Tony found a real friend there in Dr. Elfren Ramirez, a very dedicated man. He tried to help in many ways. The system in his hospital in Puerto Rico was helpful to some addicts. He'd say to them,

"If you can prove to me that for two months you can go out of here free on weekends and come back, clean, I'll give you an office of your own and make you a therapist."

He believes that by replacing narcotics with something the addict enjoys more than using drugs, he can get a man delivered from his habit. He told Tony he would put him in the University of Puerto Rico—free. His offer was a very attractive one. Tony wanted to do it very much. But he never made it back clean, not even one week during the eight months he was with Dr. Ramirez for treatment. He'd feel miserable, not because he was hooked, but because he knew he couldn't stay there in the hospital all his life. He knew he was all right there; but he also knew he would go back to the gutters of life again when he got outside.

If you go out of the hospital and shoot drugs just on weekends you can maintain yourself clean and nicely dressed. You can go dancing and dining and other things acceptable to society. But all the time Tony was using drugs, he hated it. It was like a craving he couldn't stay away from.

One day his grandmother went to New York, and she left the key to her house with Tony. He thought this would be a good time to stay there all by himself and kick his habit. The first day was all right; the second day was bad; the third day was terrible. The fourth day he ordered a large truck, and moved everything out of his grandmother's home and sold it all for dope.

Heartsick, his father shipped him back to New York. Tony was sure of himself there; after all, he had aunts in New Jersey, aunts in Brooklyn, aunts in New York City. And his mother was in New York, too. But he went from one door to another, and with tender violence, every single one of them told him,

"Get out!"

He looked so awful he couldn't even go into any store to steal; his appearance would just squeal on him. He felt he was destroyed. His family had disowned him, and he had no place to go but the streets.

He was waiting in the subway one day when a young man called his name. He looked to see who it was and recognized a boy who had cheated and stolen and shot drugs with him. But something had happened to this guy. He was clean; he was wearing a suit and a white shirt and tie, and he had a Bible in his hand. He asked Tony if he was hungry.

"I don't have any money," Tony told him.

"Let's go out and eat together," he suggested. And while they were eating, the friend told Tony all about the transforming power of God. He was talking about the change that had taken place in his own life, and how he didn't have to use drugs at all anymore, and how the problem was not in the mind, but in the soul.

Tony didn't understand a thing then, but he could at least follow his directions about getting to this little church where he would have a place to eat and sleep.

We got a bed ready for Tony at Damasco and he finished kicking his habit there over a period of nine days. Then we sent him up to Mountaindale to the camp, where he began to see what he had never seen before. He seen other addicts who would just mug you or stick you up out in the street, only now they were holding hands and praising God and praying and showing a love that he never been shown before by no one. He couldn't understand what they had, but whatever it was, he wanted it. He explained to us,

"I want what you guys have 'cause I know I'm hooked, and I want to change. I've tried everything within my own will power to change my life and nothing works. One of the worst things that can happen to a man is when he hates what he is doing but he has to continue doing it."

For four years Tony had been seeking a way, and now he could see that the answer was right in front of him. He told us,

"I didn't know what I would have to do, but I knew you people had something I didn't have, and it was something I wanted."

During Tony's seven months at camp his mind became very clear. When he was willing to come with an open heart to Jesus Christ, he repented his crimes, and Christ took his corrupted mind and put in new desires and ambitions. For the first time in his life he had something to live for. He felt he was in victory over himself. Joy and peace came to replace the craving for drugs.

One night Tony was asking God to make a way for him to move out. He was afraid to go back to the city 'cause he feared he'd head for the drugs again. He knew this fear wasn't of the Lord, and he knew he wasn't going to stay there in camp all the rest of his life either. So he said to Lennie.

"I want God's power. I need it. I'm going out to the city."

Lennie really got used by God to step out on faith and to help other boys do the same thing. He has a gift of praying for people—laying hands on them, and helping them to believe God. He was up there at Mountaindale for a long time helping the boys get that old emptiness filled up to overflowing with the Holy Spirit.

"Do you believe He will give you the power?" Lennie asked.

"Of course I believe it. I want it."

"Tony, just open your heart. Lift your hands to Him, and cry to God. Ask Him to give you all that you need."

"Here I am, Lord," Tony began. "Increase my faith. Please give me more strength."

Tony felt a sudden power coming from up high, just taking him over completely. He began to tremble, like the Philippian jailer. And something that felt like "Rivers of Living Water" were flowing through his whole body and mind. He began speaking in another tongue. He was filled with the Holy Spirit that night. This was the way God fitted Tony for his trip to the city. Lennie didn't even lay hands on him; it was the work of God.

Something happened in Tony's life, something *more* — a tremendous new experience with Christ. He was closer to God. He didn't have the fear he was talking about before. He went to the city twice that next month, and he stayed two weeks straight. But he came back victorious, and he told about the power of the Holy Spirit wherever he went. Before, we couldn't get Tony to say two words. Then suddenly we had to tell him to finish, 'cause he had so much to say about the strength of the Holy Spirit.

Tony knows, 'cause he tried so hard to make it with Dr. Ramirez in Puerto Rico, and he couldn't. Whenever he would try to stay clean by his own will power, he was always doing something else to replace the dope—drinking alcohol, taking pills, smoking pot. He had to have something else. But with Christ, the transformation was complete.

27. A Way Out

It was so great to see the guys coming one by one. The news that there was a way out for junkies was hard to believe. It traveled along the streets and into the jails, and all the time guys were coming to Damascus Church and to Mountaindale to see what it was all about. Some of them stayed; others didn't.

Pedro first found out about Christ when he was in jail. He seen six or seven guys gathering together in Riker's Island every afternoon talking about the Bible and about God. This was the fourth time Pedro had got busted and he was tired of his life the way it was. These guys had been his friends out on the street, so when they invited him to sit around with them, Pedro started listening to what they were saying about the Bible. As a junkie he was concerned like the rest of us that there was no remedy for himself; but as he read the Bible and discussed it with the other junkies, he began to feel something new in his heart—in his inner self, and he was interested. "I will try it," he said to himself, and when he came out to the street again, he went to Damascus for a day. But instead of staying there, he went back to the street, and BOOM! he was back in jail again right away!

This time he started thinking about what went wrong: "I was a fool. I should have stayed in the church where I was before, then this wouldn't have happened to me." So he served his time, and came out again to the street. His family didn't want him, and he started living on the rooftops. He was searching and thinking, "Should I go back to the church? Would that really help me?" Then one day some of the guys that knew him came to him and prayed for him, and took him with them to camp. There during his eight months away from the city, the Lord was able to get through to Pedro.

Mickey was sitting reading—all by himself—in the lobby of a New York hotel and I came through and saw him, and I could tell he was hooked. I told him I would come back and talk to him, and he stayed right there in that chair almost a whole day waiting. He didn't even go to take a shot; he just stayed sick, reading that novel until I got back to talk to him and pray for him. After we got Mickey some food and some clothes, we sent him along with a couple other addicts to a farm in West Virginia where they could kick their habits. But the funny thing is that they didn't kick at all. They didn't have to. None of them felt any pain—God delivered them completely. He saved and He healed them, all three of them.

Raul was one of them. He first experienced the love of God when he took a friend's suggestion and came in to Damascus. He was all set to rob a jewelry store when somebody told him some other guys just got through robbing it. He was all greasy dirty. He stunk to high heavens, and he was up on the rooftops, just laying there on a couple old cardboards.

He was so mad that he got up and looked through the skylight and started arguing with God,

"Why do You permit this? You're supposed to be a good God. They tell me You're a God full of love. And look at the condition I'm in . . . fourteen years addicted to heroin. Look at me! I'm filthy dirty. I stink. I can't even stand myself. Where are You? Why don't You do something?"

It was the very next day that he met this guy who told him,

"Raul, why don't you go over to this church, Damasco? Christ is there and He's delivering drug addicts."

"Uh-huh. Sure He is!"

"OK, Raul. Don't knock it. Go get high, and then come back and talk to me. I wanna tell you about this."

He did go get high and when he came back, they went over to the church together. A lady came up to Raul and she put her hand on his face, and he looked at her and saw the love of Christ coming right through her. In fact, she said, "Thank you, Lord, for bringing him in here," and Raul didn't know what to do. He saw himself all filthy and smelly, twisted out of his gall, and he couldn't figure out what this woman could be thanking God for. She asked him to stay and Raul said he would. He figured he'd get up at three in the morning and steal something and leave. But before he even went to sleep that night, he experienced the power of God coming in to change his life. And when Mom Rosado asked him if he wanted to accept Christ into his heart, he prayed after her,

"Lord, I know You're alive today and I want to accept You. Come into my life. Heal my body and transform me. I know You're able if I can only have the faith to believe."

That very night he believed God, and God came in and filled up the emptiness he had all his life. Raul was perplexed; but he was in expectation, waiting for this God he had received into his life to do something. He actually feared kicking his habit, so he asked God to take care of this for him. And his prayer was answered with a miracle. Raul felt no pains or any other trace of kicking; he can only explain it that God took it. God saved him and healed him. The moment Raul believed, God did this for him.

28. The Romance

Seems like God moves in on each one of us in just a little different way. Like Jerry, for instance, it was a constant battle with him. Push. Push. Push. Then one day it seemed as though the wine had mellowed and it was just right for him to do what God wanted him to do.

Jerry's little old Orthodox Jewish mother took me aside after he'd been home with her a week, and she asked me,

"What about this Jesus?" She's getting curious.

Why? Because everything's different with Jerry. Now, instead of forcing her to beg for him, he comes home and knocks on the door,

"Ma? It's me, Ma. It's Jerry."

And she opens the door and Jerry wraps his big arms around her and holds her close to him. And he caresses her hair and kisses her, and says,

"Look, Ma. It's all over with now. Jesus Christ came into my life."

She hurries around getting supper. She lights the candles on Friday night, and uses her special dishes; and after supper Jerry tells her to sit down and rest. He clears off the table, and he washes the dishes up and sweeps the floor. He may go out and buy her a newspaper or an ice cream cone.

Another thing she notices, and she laughed as she told me,

"You know, Jerry even washes the tub out after he takes a bath."

These things may seem like trivia to some people, nothing. But after thirteen horrible years they mean everything. And we all know it's Jesus living in Jerry, not Jerry. Like some of us do these things for a wife, a brother, out of obligation; we know well we should do something. But these new things we're doing are exciting; they happen out of our hearts, out of a tremendous desire to show this wonderful love that's lifted us into really living!

No wonder people get curious about what's happened. No wonder they start wondering, "What about this Jesus?"

If we had it all to do over again — to go through the grief, the misery, the anguish, the mental hospitals, the jails — if we had to live again through every bitter experience in order to find Jesus Christ, we'd go right through the whole mess. Knowing Him is worth every horrible hour we spent. God has a purpose in mind. God has a reason for life.

I suppose we're the ones who hold Him off. We come to God; but all people come always with a little reservation, and when that reservation leaves, it's noticeable. Something really happens to your whole life. You get turned around—all the way around.

Maybe the addict comes, kind of like he would go to the hospital to lay up for a while, to get a new hold on himself. When you start this way you do what you can—you come. You give as much of yourself as you can to this God you can't see. You stop using drugs, you stop smoking and drinking, you stop cursing, you stop hating — at least you start to stop all these things because you start to taste a new kind of delicious love. And you get hungry to be with this new Lover who's not like any human being you ever known. He's the only One you ever met who fills up that awful empty feeling you've had as far back as you can remember.

You eat and think and sleep and dream about this Christ, who has promised never ever to leave you. His new love gets down inside you and is just quietly working away and working away. Until finally in one clear bright moment of total recognition you see that without this Love, this presence of God inside you, you're nothing. The only thing you can do by yourself is destroy yourself.

This is the moment when the spirit, the mind, the body and the heart all say, "OK, Jesus. Take over!" It's a beautiful thing to watch the change in a person — just like a calm, an order, a peacefulness that comes over him. You can notice it in his actions, in the way he goes out towards others. With us, we notice it in the way we feel about each other. We've found a love that makes us behave differently than we ever did before. We've found a love that makes us concerned about each other. Maybe someone's late getting in—I go out at two o'clock in the morning looking for one of the boys who's going through some trial. We're constantly on the lookout for each other. You see, we always have to be watching, watching, 'cause the Devil is here all the time looking for a chance to fool us again. He's a constant enemy. He never lets up. All the time temptation is right behind us.

God has to keep at us. This Christian life takes a long time to develop. Like Paul says, it's a race we run. It's a process. We fight and we fight and we got to get hit along the way. As ex-addicts we say, "Well, we're growing in the Lord." But at the same time we may try to get, say, a little closer to the kitchen to weasel our way into a little extra chow. These are the tendencies from before, and some of them hang around a long time — some guys have them more than others.

We're still in this body, and He's going to polish up this old guy that He started on; but it's a long race, and a hard fight, and it takes a constant polishing, polishing, polishing. It's going to be a long hard process, and many people won't stand for it. But when this thing happened to me, I knew this was the way I must go. You see, where else could I go? The words that they gave me at Damascus and Mountaindale have worked out to be truly Words of Life. I was dead, and now, man! I'm living! It's as simple as that.

Before when I had a problem, I would kill it with a shot of dope. Now when temptations come, I call on Christ—and you learn to call immediately! He forgives us so much! That's why we love Him so much. Temptations do come—often and heavy, because of my past. The desires of my body cry out. But I land on the guy and I say, "Come now. Come on!" And I call — sometimes right out loud, "Jesus!" when it gets so much. Sometimes I say, "Lord, get this cross off my back!" One of the fellows comes with a problem about his wife; another guy comes with this or that; my daughter's got a problem in school; they're running here; this guy needs . . . Oh! it's like a storm, till finally I fall down and say,

"Please, God. I can't do it. Please, You do it!"

And it works out fine. He takes over and steers the ship, and boy! It's beautiful! He's the Captain; He's in command. And the joy comes, and the radiance, because you feel the power of God just generating up through you. You start talking to someone and you feel Him. It's wonderful. This always happens to me when I get involved in a conversation about Jesus. I get excited. Man! It's just joy coming out. Some people I talk to, I just look at them. I can feel Him, and they seem so out of it, and I wonder, "What's wrong? Don't you know Jesus?" There's such a difference between knowing about God, and knowing God.

"I knew about Christ before," Rudy told me. "I could read the Bible and get sort of a little revelation out of it, but it was sort of like looking at a picture without knowing the whole story. Then when the

Holy Ghost came into me, I met Jesus Christ as a person. It seemed like I actually shook hands with Him—it was no second-hand experience. I could see Him and know Him as a real person, and I could love Him. Ever since I got baptized with the Holy Spirit it's been different for me. I can go out on the street, and into the bars, and tell the junkies and the winos that there is a way out for them; I can tell them about Christ and not be afraid. In my life the baptism of the Holy Spirit was a different experience from salvation. It increased my understanding and my love. There was something new in me."

When our boys talk about the Holy Spirit of God moving into their ragged lives, Brother! They know it from fact, from experience. They know *Jesus!* You know, before, we'd shoot people, hit 'em over the head. We just didn't care about them and how they felt. Now, if we even talk cross to somebody and they get offended, we feel bad. This is what Christ said—that if we even say something hateful to a person, it's the same thing as murdering them. We just wanna go around and do good to people, and help them.

I get up now in the morning and I see the trees, and at night I look up and see the stars; and I see people, and I feel for them. When God comes to your heart, you look at people and you see everybody pretty, and you love them so much. This is beautiful, because I know it's not me. It's Christ in me that does this. Even when I try to explain it all to people, it's not me; the Lord gives me the words. The Lord has changed our very lives, our very beings. Being born again is something that really happened to us. We were lost and alone, and now we're inside, and we want to thank Him for finding us with every breath we take, with every act of our lives.

29. Every Day . . . A New Experience

Being constantly with our Christian brothers is a big help. As we seek for righteousness, our minds get more keen, our hearts get more love. He blesses our lives together because we believe there is no limit to the power of God. We must be reminded every day of what we believe. Hearing the Word of God, and hearing the glad praise of our brothers keeps us in a good growing atmosphere, and our desire to do something for God gets bigger and bigger.

The most important time for all of us seemed to be while we was traveling in our truck. One guy starts reading the Bible, and he finds something and yells out,

"Dig this, man! Look what the Lord put down here."

Then another guy will come on, and this guy breaks out preaching a sermon on it. It's a beautiful thing—so free. And we get so much out of the Bible—more than if somebody'd told us we had to read it! And then we start praying, and we go riding along praising God and thanking Him, and asking Him for the next meeting, or a buddy who is still addicted, or money for supper, or just anything we need. We learn this way. We got a hunger for God.

All the time He was there; He just had to wait till we stopped running around and turned around to let Him touch us. Now we ask for something and He gives us double! He's wonderful! We got a whole new family—Family of God! We get up there in a church, and when I introduce Frankie he tells about how he never had no mother or father, and he grins,

"See these guys here? They my brothers; I got fat ones and skinny ones, light ones and dark ones."

Then he looks out at the people in the audience and he says,

"And I got mothers and fathers — that's what you are to me! Family of God. Wow!"

God saved Frankie to be Frankie—happy and gay, like He planned him to be; He saved him to be himself. When I introduce him after the drama's over, he comes out and the people clap, 'cause he goes through a lot of rough stuff in that play. And he'll grin and say,

"Them claps should be for Jesus! He done it!"

We all learned the suffering of life in what they call a jungle, jumping here, ducking there. We didn't recognize God in anybody 'cause we were just trying to use people. We were hungry, starving, nothing. We needed God in every way. So when He came to us He really came! WOW! Every day is a new experience walking hand in hand with Christ.

30. Sombra

It's a mystery what turns up with the different guys during the shakedown process following conversion. God's got His own way for each one of us. We help each other as much as we can. And it's really strange some of the things He does for us when we let go of that little bit of ourselves that keeps His power from flowing through us.

Sombra's story appeared in the San Juan newspapers in 1964. But it started back before that. Sombra grew up in Puerto Rico where his father was a conductor on a train. He used to help him collect the tickets, and go to parties with him. When he was eleven, his father died and his mother remarried. He didn't want to have to face a stepfather because he loved his own father very much, so he left. Later, sentenced to 35 years for a robbery, he heard the inmates say, "If you try drugs, you'll forget everything." Years later in New York he had twenty bags of heroin hoarded up to take his own life. He got up from his bed to cook up a giant overdose, and suddenly he saw a cross of light in front of him. He didn't know what it meant, but he was frightened and he ran out of the room and down the street. When he came to Prospect Avenue and 162nd Street, he saw a cross outside a building. "Maybe this is God trying to tell me something," he thought, so he walked inside the building and kneeled down at the altar and started to pray.

The reason he had wanted to take his own life was that he felt disgusted, rejected. His family didn't want him; his friends despised him. It just wasn't worth it to go on living. Sombra had been to four prisons in Puerto Rico for smuggling whiskey, for fighting to defend his girl, for stealing. He was in eight prisons in the United States for dope charges. The whole police force was looking for him in Puerto Rico because he was so well-known for his crimes.

For two weeks Sombra kept coming back to Damasco, trying to get a place to stay. But for one reason or another he never could make it—the office would be closed, or they had just taken in several others for the night, and there was no more room. Then one day about five of us guys were praying at the church and we remembered that little skinny guy who'd been coming around just too late. We decided the next time we seen him, we'd snatch him.

Sure enough, he came to the service; and when we asked him to stay he said yes. He went home and got some clothes and came back to kick his habit. He was thin and undernourished; he weighed only 75 pounds! He was so weak he had to stay in bed for five days after we took him in; but the boys would carry him down to the services. Every night he asked for somebody to come and help him down to the temple. Then one night when the preacher gave the altar call, he asked to be carried to the front. He had such determination.

"Either I'm going to find God, or I'm going to die in this place."

Even the first day he told us he felt God was reaching him. The guys would take turns carrying his food up to him; and after five days he began to gain strength. After a while at Mountaindale Sombra's weight got back up to his original 135 pounds. He was always a little guy and he had escaped so often from the prisons, gotten out of tight places so readily, the police called him "The Shadow."

While he was up there in the country, Sombra heard God telling him he should go back to Puerto Rico and give himself up to the police. He began talking to Mom Rosado about it, and she took it up with a number of influential people—ministers and lawyers. A number of ministers who had known Sombra since his conversion, and had heard him preach, wrote letters of recommendations for him to the Puerto Rican authorities. Much ground work was done before they left New York. Then when everything was as set as it could be, Mom went with Sombra to San Juan. Word went ahead of them that "The Shadow" was returning. When they arrived, they went together to the court in San Juan and Sombra walked up to the judge and gave himself up. The judge was a Christian believer, and when he looked at Sombra and heard him talk, he saw such a changed man that he permitted him to go home that night rather than putting him into the jail.

He asked Sombra two questions: "First, why did you escape?" And second, "Why have you come to give yourself up?"

To answer the first question, Sombra told the judge that he had gotten his drug habit in prison; but he couldn't get enough stuff there to support it. The pains got so bad after he was hooked that he was constantly looking for a way to escape and find more drugs. He was well-trusted by the prison officials—when they see you doing good for a long time they give you special jobs. They didn't realize Sombra was hooked, so they sent him one day to work on the prison farm. The guard was with him, but he fell asleep, and Sombra took the chance to get out.

In answer to the second question, "Why have you come to give yourself up?" Sombra said,

"I have found Christ, and since that time I have wanted to be a preacher of the Word. The only way I can be a preacher is by first paying my debt to society."

Escapees are automatically thrown into solitary confinement, but the district attorney talked three different times with Sombra, and said,

"This man can be trusted. Give him a place to work in the office."

This was the chief D.A. for the entire district, and he had much influence. Mom Rosado prayed with the D.A. that day, and he became a tremendous help to Sombra. He was already a believer, but his own faith became greatly strengthened through this experience.

The first day Sombra was back, his old buddies—some of them are there for eternity! — came to talk with him. There are 4000 in this presidio (state prison). Out in the yard during recreation time some of them asked how he'd managed to stay out of jail for six years, and he told them the story of how he had made his escape and gone to the United States. He told them how he started stealing, getting dope, how he was arrested ten or twelve times by the police — in Terre Haute, Indiana; Lewisburg, Pennsylvania; Louisville, Kentucky. Then he went on to tell how he returned to New York, and how God had led him to Damasco. The prisoners listened and watched. They could see this was not the same "Shadow" they had known so well in the old days, and they could tell he was not putting them on. Because of the new Sombra, some of them believed in Jesus Christ right away; others lingered in the background, just watching. The chief of all chaplains in the Puerto Rican prisons, Sally Olson, saw what was happening among the men, and she turned over her pulpit to Sombra. He had special meetings three times a week; through these meetings men continued to come to Christ right there inside the prison.

Sombra's case came to the attention of many people, even the governor of the island, Muñoz Marin. Prisoners usually come to court in handcuffs and prison garb; but Sombra dressed as a minister—in a black suit, white shirt and tie. He appeared in court about eight times during the twenty days of trial. Mom Rosado would come by in her car and pick him up and drive him to the court. She made a very striking picture in the courtroom with her red hair, and her black suit with a high collar. Her name, Leoncia, means "lioness," and she proved many times over to be one of God's real royal line. She went every inch of the way with Sombra in his attempt to pay his debt to society.

The last day the courtroom was full of people — inside and outside—newspaper reporters and photographers covered the case almost every day during the trial. Lots of curious people came to see the outcome. The judge looked at Sombra and asked him,

"Guilty, or not guilty?"

"Guilty," Sombra answered, "but I've been transformed."

"Why did you give yourself up?"

"Because God has given me a call to preach, but I can't go out for Him until I've paid my debt to society. I come depending on the wisdom and faithfulness of God."

The judge looked very solemn, and then pronounced:

"After hearing the sincerity of this man, and hearing of his desire to work for other people and to help society; and now especially with the great drug problem we have here in Puerto Rico, I feel he could be a great asset to our people, to our country. Upon observing the transformation in his life we hereby dismiss all cases pending against him, and absolve him of the charges against him. We place him in the hands of Reverend Leoncia Rosado, so that he may return immediately to New York to take care of his affairs. I also recommend that this young man be given a card that will give him entry into the prisons of the island, so that he may carry on the same good work as he has during his stay here in San Juan."

It was October 17, 1964, but the court wrote into the record that the day he had escaped—June 12, 1959, was the same day he had returned voluntarily to give himself up. This technically blotted out five years of offense against the government; it was the only way he could be pardoned under Puerto Rican law.

Sombra spent about four months in New York before he went back to Puerto Rico. There he ministered in the prisons nearly a year among addicts. Then, on his return to the States he joined us in Chicago to help us with the drama.

31. Talk About Love!

When we come home to God we get loved like we never been loved before by anyone. We can walk with our heads up, and a smile on our faces. Little things that happen during a day make us call out, "Thank you, Jesus!" or "Praise the Lord!" When we get a parking spot in the city, or somebody brings in a loaf of homemade bread, or one of the guys falls into a blessing, it's, "Thank you, thank you, thank you, Lord!"

Since we discovered that God really loves us, and it don't matter any more all the terrible things we done, then we got to try to help other people make the same discovery we made. We can go into all kinds of places now—like in the rescue missions. We see the bums there and we cry with them. We know what it feels like to be lost. We can speak with them,

"I know how you feel. I lived this life."

We can see the wonderful possibilities in a person now. In a girls' prison, for instance, we can tell them God loves and cares for them, and a couple of girls will come to accept the Lord. We can see ahead what God has for them — they can be fit mothers and loving wives. We know that God can do this for them, because He has done so much for us.

Many times as we travel, Terry comes across some colored people, and he can say to them,

"I know what you're going through, but don't worry about it

because God cares. He's no respecter of persons. He loves you."

Then he began to discover that people hate what they don't understand. They're afraid. Now God has given him compassion. Many times when we go as a group into some restaurant, someone will say to Terry,

"I'm sorry but we can't serve you."

And he just quietly answers, "Fine. I'll find someplace else."

And he doesn't hate them for it. He's learned to not resent it anymore. Terry don't worry now when he's in a white neighborhood or a colored neighborhood. He's learned to trust God. He belongs to Him. He no longer seeks his own recognition; he don't have to defend Terry no more. Terry has found his place. This is what God can do—for anybody. It doesn't matter how old or how young they are. Only God can make this kind of change in a man's heart and mind.

The greatest need of any human being anywhere is love. That's how God made us. And when we know that God loves us, then everything changes — the way we feel about ourselves, about other people, about everything. It was love that Raul felt when Mom Rosado looked at him—all filthy—and touched his face and thanked God for him. Love is what I felt when Pop Rosado was standing at the door that night at 11:30 when I came tearing back to the church. Love is what we all feel when we stand around after a service and thank God for changing our lives. The most important message in the world is just three words—God is love. He loves and loves and loves and loves . . . .

This is kind of like giving a guy a rifle after he's been trained. When you get the Holy Spirit to be the love and the power inside of you, He puts the bullets into the gun and you can go out and fight the enemy. Our eyes have been opened, and our minds. My heart readily accepts it all now — there's been a change. I love people. Chuck used to cut people when he was angry; now he can go out and look at people and love them so much. Strangers he just looks at, and he loves them more than his own brothers. God does something in his heart when he looks at people — everybody looks pretty. We thank God for making us love people, because we didn't used to love. Now we want to help them more than anybody could possibly help. We walk down the street, or sit in the restaurant, and we see a junkie, and we know it right away. Or we see a wino staggering down the street. Or some guy stops us for two bits, or wants to bum a weed. And we know that God loves these people, that Jesus died for them. And more than anything else we want to tell them, "God loves you, man! Do you know that God loves you? Do you know what that love will do for you? Listen, Man—*God* loves *you!* God loves *you*!"

God's love ain't the soft, mushy, sentimental kind though. We love the guys; but sometimes we have to take a stick across the knuckles—real good and hard. With a child you treat him as a child; with a man you treat him as a man. Some guys are the type that can weasel their way into anybody's heart. We see it; we know it; it happens many times. This kind of a guy you need to strike quick, and make him to grow. And the only way he'll grow is by putting him in a place where he has to fight.

Sometimes I almost have to become an opponent in order to make the guys react. Sometimes the only way I can get Frankie to really act in the play is to actually hit him in one of the scenes instead of just pretending to. Sometimes I have to get Ronnie mad before he'll really work to give the best performance. He gets mad and shows us how good he can do it. Actually, the Holy Spirit helps us shape each other up. Nobody holds a grudge about it. We come off after the drama and everybody stands with their arms around each other thanking God and saying, "Man! That was beautiful!" In the process of growing, we feel the love; we know God is dealing with us. It's beautiful!

One of the guys was giving us a hard time on the road. He's a man; he's no child. But he's lost as far as direction is concerned. He wants to make it, but he keeps going backwards. He's got no victory. One morning he was sneaking around grumbling and making trouble for everyone. I had to take an all-the-way measure.

"OK. Pack. Leave."

Right away there's a reaction that sets in. The Holy Spirit is there. He's dealing; and He brings to mind what would be the outcome if he left in the condition he was in. So God fixes it that when one of us reaches our limit, another one comes in to take over. I done all I could. But when Jerry saw what had happened, he got in there. So all things work out fine. This guy didn't pack; he didn't leave. But this is what has to happen sometimes. God works; and we see that it's all for the better. This way we grow; God is always giving us one more chance, one more chance. He says His mercy is from everlasting to everlasting.

Some places we go they got a rule. You break it? Out you go! It's a rule; you broke it, so you got to leave. If God was like that we would all be in trouble. That's the way I was that time in Mountaindale though, when they hauled me up in front of the congregation and called me a Pharisee. I learned this thing the hard way, but I'm glad I learned it. There's no rules that we as human beings have made that we do not break in order to help a soul to the Kingdom of God. I don't believe there's a rule anywhere that is worth more than a soul.

Sure, we make rules; and if there's no excuse to break them, we don't break them. But there's one reason we do have for breaking any rule. That's the winning of a human being to the Lord.

Learning to win other people who were in the same kind of tight spot we knew so long was a problem too. Pee Wee, for instance, had a desire to tell people about Christ; it was his constant prayer that God would touch the fellows he seen nodding on the street. He'd say,

"Lord, look upon those that are lost like I was." But he wasn't able to do anything more than that.

Then in Chicago he seen the need and he began to go out in faith and speak to some of the junkies who needed comfort. He tells them he used to be just like they are, that there is a way out, a way to get clean, and God is the way. He takes them for coffee, walks the street with them, brings them in to lunch with some of the rest of us, listens to them, prays with them. He holds onto them day after day. You got to do that. It's one thing to tell someone that Jesus saves, or God loves; but if you aren't showing the love of God to them, your talk don't mean much. An alcoholic who came to us later said,

"Terry made me feel like a real man. He put his arm around me and gave me a kiss on the cheek."

If Terry hadn't felt this real human concern for him, he might not have been interested in the love of God. We soon find out we can't fake it — we can't give away something we don't have. If we don't have love, we can't give love.

We encourage the boys to make their own rules for getting hooked up with God. We get so excited about the things we find in the Scriptures that the preaching and the praying just take off any place, any time. Raul and Tony D. and Wayne and several others been to Bible Institute now and they can teach. Juggy takes off regularly just preaching out of the heart of God. He's good at it, but he wants to go to a good school to learn how to really work for God. Riding in the truck, sitting around the table, working on various projects, we sing, and pray, and talk. We learn this way.

Some of those guys stay up till two, three o'clock in the morning studying the Bible. Pee Wee and Chuck stay out in the street and just talk to people about the love of God. After the drama, guys go out to eat together. Yeah, we have a rule that says we should be in at a certain time, but we stretch it! Lights should be out, but when there's something more important, I'm not gonna tell them to go to sleep. As long as they get up in the morning—let them go ahead and study and testify and all that. They have this hunger for the Word of God and a concern for others, and I'm glad. I wouldn't want it any other way.

32. The Reality

By the fall of 1965 the drama was stirring interest in many places in the United States, and as far away as the Philippines. We had enough demand to form our second group of eight guys to go on the road with the play. We got our name, "The Addicts," painted on two microbuses and set out in two different directions. People are always curious wherever we go. If they're addicts they come to ask us what we're doing, and the Lord has let us help hundreds of junkies this way. If they're not addicts, they want to know what we're doing. So we get a chance to tell what God has done for us either way.

Of course, this growing — each one of us, and the drama groups too — means problems to face. We never been over this road before, and it sure is "under construction." Some of the bumps are pretty hard; some of the questions take a long time to answer. But the Lord is faithful. He keeps His word. And we know this with all our hearts!

We got two kinds of things to figure out. First, we think about what we're going to do with the new life God gave us, where we going to live, what kind of work we should do, if we should get married. Each guy got to meditate on that himself. The other kind has to do with the group, the drama, the prophecy, the calls that come to us for help in other cities.

Many places we put on the drama, people beg us to stay and help them with the drug problem in their city. In Chicago we have a local work with some of our boys in charge. Tony and Juggy stayed several months in Vancouver, B.C., after we put the play on out there. Baltimore wanted us to start a work for addicts. Denver is another city we are concerned about.

Now we have four groups of ex-addicts on the road — thirty-two men, completely transformed by the power of God. We are seeing the prophecy fulfilled: "I will send you throughout the world." In less than two years we were traveling all over the United States from coast to coast. All faiths are receiving us—Methodist, Baptist, Presbyterian, Episcopalian, Catholic, Pentecostal, Lutheran. And campuses—Baylor University in Texas, Connecticut State Teacher's College, North Park College in Chicago. It seems to work this way wherever we go. The bookings in a town open up other things—radio, television, people with problems. We been traveling, sleeping in church basements and homes of Christian people. We put on the drama, and take an offering. That gets us to the next place, and some of it we put to helping girl addicts who come to Christ in our meetings. We've had a lot of them, and we can't take them with us on the road, and we don't want to just leave them in the same old place where they been hooked. For a while we had a farm in West Virginia; then, we got a house in the Chicago area. But we need a place out in the country away from the city temptations, where girls can go to grow in their new life.

One girl, 20 years old, came to West Virginia with her sister. We'll call her Susi. She wrote to Jerry,

> "Kathie and I have decided you're our papa in Christ. We probably love you more than we do our own father.
>
> Praise the Lord for another day! Things are coming along just fine here, thank God! Kathie and I went to Mt. Airy to testify for the King. It was beautiful! I've never been so happy in all my life.
>
> Jeri is back on drugs. We called a pastor and with God's help he's going to try to bring her back to us here. Satan really uses that 'monkey,' doesn't he? But Jesus will beat Satan!
>
> Love in Christ,
>
> SUSI"

A sixteen-year-old girl from Connecticut who kicked her habit when she came to Christ wrote,

> "I'm really content and happy. I have found so much peace of mind with the Lord. My only desire is to let the world know about Jesus Christ. The devil comes and we do have our trials and tribulations, but we fight the devil. I love the Lord. He is the only answer.
>
> I miss you! All the guys and you will be in my prayers

constantly! May the Lord Jesus Christ keep you in His arms forever.

Love,
J."

Panels on television give us fantastic liberty to tell what is happening to us. Norman Ross, on his "Off The Cuff" program in Chicago, even asked us to close the two hours of conversation with prayer! Broadcasters ask us in for radio interviews. Hospitals, jails, high school auditoriums, service clubs open their doors to us. A group of guys went to London, England; we been asked to Hong Kong, Finland, Germany, Canada, South Africa. There's no end. We don't understand it all. Everything just keeps moving. God is keeping His word. He's faithful. I believe this with all my heart. Whoever thought them breezy guys nodding on the stoops of the Bronx would ever be on TV! Or in a movie, or on a record, or in a book! But God has opened all these doors to us, and we never know what's going to happen another day.

Schools are the best place to go, we think, because we get the chance to show young kids the terrible life of a drug addict. Most schools will tell us we can't bring in any denomination into our talk. They tell us,

"Go ahead and talk about how you were on drugs, and how you got in jail, and what happened there. Tell the horrors of drug addiction, the awful life lived on the rooftops, the way your physical body gets destroyed."

When we get through with that, somebody always asks,

"Are you on drugs now?"

"No."

"Then how did you stop?"

At that point we are forced to tell them that God filled up our emptiness. And once we start talking about Christ, they forget their warning to us. We find it better to give an example to them instead of preaching anyway. We don't talk about denominations; we don't talk about churches. The Bible tells us that we are the temples of the Holy Ghost; so we just tell them about what has happened inside of us.

It was really something when we got invited to send some of the boys to London, England, for the world conference of the Full Gospel Businessmen's Fellowship.

Everybody was sending to Puerto Rico, to New York for their birth certificates. Frankie sent to Puerto Rico for his, and one day Jerry brought a letter in to him from the Department of Health. Frankie looked at me and said,

"Johnny, I'm not going."

He had a feeling. The letter was in Spanish, so he brought it over to me to read. It said they couldn't find any record of Frankie's birth in all the records in San Juan. They even went to the hospitals and everywhere to try to find his name, but no good—they couldn't find it.

Frankie's heart fell. We left him alone. He wanted so much at least to find out his mother's name, his father's name, where he was born. Because all he ever knew was that his mom died on the delivery table when he was born. He felt real bad.

He was sitting there by himself and his heart kept saying,

"But I wanna know!"

And the Spirit just came to him and told him something,

"God has your record, Frankie. Even the day of the beginning of this world He got your record. He knows when you were born. He knows the day, the minute, the hour, the second. Whether it was daytime or nighttime."

And Frankie came to find the rest of us, and we could tell before he said anything that he was all right.

"Fellows," he said, "ya don't hafta worry! Upstairs they got my record!"

Then that night in the service Frankie told the people to have special prayer for him, because he really did want to know. He was thinking, "Upstairs they got my record, but that's upstairs. Down here's a whole different world. I need it down here too, Lord."

So we all prayed. And you know what? The next trip to the office in McKeesport, Fred got a whole bunch of letters to give out, and there was one from Puerto Rico for Frankie. It was his birth certificate. Now he knows his father's name — Porfirio. "That's a boss name," Frankie says. "It's Frank in English." And he's got the place he was born—Ponce. "That's one of the biggest," Frankie says. His mother's name they don't got. Someday he thinks he'll go down to Puerto Rico and find out all the things he wants to know about the family he never had. In the meantime, little old Frankie—the dirty little orphan that used to break into Bronx apartments and wish he had a key of his own so he could walk in the front door like a real man — has a key of his own now and comes home from work in Chicago to an apartment of his own. God's got Frankie in His hand.

The Lord Jesus has lifted us up; He's taken like the foolish things of the world to confound the wise. Because we are ex-drug addicts, we have special weaknesses. People know this and they watch us close. We have to walk circumspectly, to be unspotted. It's strange in a way. In the dope world we would go all the way, too — either you shot dope, or you didn't. Now in our new life we have to go all the way — either we belong to God or we don't. We can't make it if we try to serve two masters.

We keep reminding each other that if it wasn't for Jesus Christ we'd still be shooting dope. He's lifted me up that I may lift Him up. This is our nourishment, that we are able to witness to other people about His love. And when we tell them about Jesus they get nourished too. I have to pray every day that the Lord will keep me remembering what He has taken me from. "Lord, keep me humble." If the words I speak are my words, they don't give life. The only way we get life is through Jesus. The only way we give life is through Jesus. Jesus Christ is reality.

33. Higher Than High

It was two o'clock in the morning before I turned out the light to go to sleep. I lay there in the dark trying to get things straight in my mind. It wasn't easy for me to see some of the guys leaving the group to go their own way. They're like my own kids, you know. Sure, I know all of them got to find their own special spot; I know all the guys can't be in the drama all the time. But I couldn't help feeling a little bit sorry for myself now that the hustle of the day was over, and everything was dark and still.

Things seemed to be happening so fast. There were so many directions to go, so many decisions to be made right now. And the guys from the original group was taking on new responsibilities and lots of times couldn't be around when I needed them.

Louis was one. He was married to a beautiful girl from Los Angeles. Man! We'll never forget their wedding. All of us were in Chicago at the time. I guess it made every guy feel a lot closer to his personal dreams, when we seen Louis capture such a lovely trophy. He had his wife with him in Chicago and he had a job. She was working too.

Now Dannie's married too. Dannie, who never had any problem about his color, married a girl from the west, and took her back to New York with him. He got along just great the summer before that, too. Worked in a camp for poor kids off the streets of New York. I remembered how scared he was—didn't know if he could make it with all those college kids being counselors and all. But pretty soon they was coming to Dannie for help, "How would you handle this kid, Dan? He does . . . . " He got a lot of confidence through that job, learned to trust the Holy Spirit in the tight spots of a day.

Yeah, I was glad the guys were finding their own happiness. But the Devil was working overtime on me, whispering at me, "They're all leavin' you, Johnny. Frankie and Louis and Julio all got jobs now. They don't care no more. Better watch out, Johnny."

Then there was the farm for the new fellows. It's important to get them out of the city fast — away from the old neighborhood. Three times we had to move the guys who were kicking their habits, once in the middle of the night, before we found this house out in the country south of Chicago, where nobody was complaining. Man! it was great! But now the neighbors out there were scaring each other with rumors about the addicts going back to their old ways. They feared for the safety of their children; so we were being evicted.

One of the newspapers said, "Their ideals are wonderful. We have no quarrel with their motives, but this is not where they belong . . . . Why should we take the slums of Chicago out here?"

Always there is a shadow of the past hanging over a junkie's head. Pee Wee and Tommy and Rudy worked so hard getting these guys in off the street and cleaned up. Now what could we do with nineteen of them?

I couldn't help but smile in the dark as I thought of Pee Wee's butterfly story. When he first started serving God he felt he needed a wife—somebody to be close to him, to help him. He prayed for just the right girl. He always thought she would be down in the island where he spent such a happy time as a little kid. So he and a friend bought round trip tickets to San Juan, and Pee Wee told his family before he left, "I'm going back home to get married." When the two weeks were gone the friend says,

"Well, I guess we better get back to New York."

"I'm not leaving," Pee Wee said. " 'Cause I haven't found my wife yet, and I know God brought me here for that purpose."

In Bayamon he met two sisters who used to talk with him and go to church with him. One of them was very beautiful, and Pee Wee was proud to be seen with her. The other was pretty but quiet and very humble, and Pee Wee always saw something in her that was different from other girls. Now he thought he was getting close to finding his wife, but he didn't know which way to move. So he prayed,

"Now I don't know what to do, God. I don't know which one You got picked out for me."

One day Pee Wee was sitting in the living room with the family—the mother, the two sisters, and a few other people. He was looking at the humble one and meditating,

"Lord, you know I don't want to make a mistake."

All of a sudden a butterfly come in through the open window, and it floated round and round the room. Pee Wee's heart was fluttering like the butterfly—when God talks to you He doesn't talk in your ear, He talks in your heart. And Pee Wee felt like God was telling him,

"Wherever the butterfly lands, she will be your wife."

He didn't want to hold back, and then tell people later that God had spoken to him, so he says out loud,

"God just spoke to me in my heart, and He told me that when that butterfly lands on somebody, I got to tell that person something."

Everybody kind of stopped talking and watched the butterfly. It swooped around the room several more times and came to rest silently on the shoulder of the humble sister.

Pee Wee walked over to her and whispered in her ear,

"You're going to be my wife."

I thought about Carmen now—and her new life with Pee Wee. She was a grade school teacher in Puerto Rico. Now, together in Chicago, she and Pee Wee were walking the streets, talking to junkies and showing them the love of Jesus Christ.

I thought about Terry, and how hard he was working on his biology so he could get enough points for a general education diploma. And Cheche, who wants to study music—he plays for the drama—practices for hours when he gets near a piano. Louis is good at art — he'd like to go on to art school. And Tony'd like to get ready to go into social work. Juggy's looking for the best place to learn to be a preacher. I laughed out loud—Juggy went the other day to get his driver's license and couldn't even parallel park, he got so busy telling the instructor about the Lord!

Suddenly the sound of the telephone scattered my thoughts, and I rolled over and grabbed it to my ear. A woman's voice was stiff with fear,

"Johnny, please come. Right away. Curtis took an overdose. I think he's dying."

Jerry and I tumbled into our trousers and went down to the second floor where one of our new boys was staying. Curtis was one of Pee Wee's converts — he spent hours and days and nights with him. We thought Curtis had made it. Now as we opened the door, we saw him lying on the floor. Jerry began breathing in his mouth and I started to massage his chest. It was an old familiar picture — we'd been in it many times, in both roles.

All the time we prayed — desperately, and from time to time, out loud. We knew God wanted Curtis to make it; but He'd have to pull him through; it looked like he was gone. We turned him over and a terrible mess of blood and vomit poured out his mouth. We laid him gently on the bed, and all the time I was thinking,

"Why is it so hard for some? Why do some of us make it and other guys fail?"

Jerry left to get some salt for an injection, and I continued artificial respiration. Finally Curtis began to breathe; the salt shot stimulated his heart action. Life began to flow back ever so faintly. Jerry and I were both scared. We knew if the cops came in on us now we had a very good chance of getting busted. We didn't know what that might mean. We asked Curtis' wife to give us ten minutes' headstart before she called the police for an ambulance to take her husband to the hospital. Jerry and I walked back to our room wondering if Curtis would get another chance, or if this was curtains for him. One boy did die the other day — they said it was a heart attack, but we aren't sure.

Before we went to sleep we called the hotel desk and asked for Room 202. The clerk told us the occupant just got carried out on a stretcher. We called the closest hospital and they said Curtis was there — in a deep coma.

We didn't doubt God's love for Curtis. We did question where we maybe failed in helping him. Most of the time he would come in around noon and we'd invite him to eat lunch with us. We were speaking about the Lord and praising Him like we always did, but I didn't know whether Curtis was listening or not. Pee Wee often prayed with him,

"Touch his heart, God. And keep him. Protect him, and give him another chance to know You."

And Curtis would go out, and come back again the next day. He reminded me of myself—all the suffering I had felt. And the longing. And the times I walked into places looking for something—I didn't know what it was. We told him our experiences—all we went through. And we told him how Christ was the One we had found, and how Christ was the One he was looking for.

He kept coming back but he didn't seem to be able to make up his mind. He was on dope and he was hooked. I remembered one day how he walked out, and then he come back again, and then he left. That same day about 5:30 it was his wife that walked in asking for Pee Wee,

"You know something? My husband comes home and talks about Pee Wee—the one who is always telling him about the love of God."

She had just seen Curtis as she come home from work, and he took ten dollars away from her.

"I can't take it any longer," she started to cry. "That's why I came here. If nothing in here could change his life I gotta leave him. I can't do anymore for him, but I can't go on this way. So if there's anything you can do for me, please do it."

I remembered how Pee Wee sat down with her right there and told her about Lazarus in the Bible,

"This man was dead and he couldn't do nothing for himself. He couldn't get over to where Jesus was because he was dead. But his sister went to Jesus and told him that her brother was dead. And Jesus loved them both so much He came over to where Lazarus was, and raised him from the dead.

"Your husband is dead too, and he can't do nothing for himself. The Bible says, 'Believe in the Lord and you and your house will be saved.' And Pee Wee told her, 'Maybe you are the one who needs salvation right now, so you can help Curtis come alive."

I remembered the night she got baptized with the Holy Spirit. And the night the two of them came back to the church together. Curtis was crying and he wanted to turn himself over to the Lord. We prayed with him and talked with him. Then we began to take him with us when we put on the drama or held a service. I remembered how Curtis left with one of the groups that traveled as far west as Denver. That was really something — he never been much of any place but Chicago before.

What happened? I wondered as I rolled over. The morning light was streaking through the cracked shade. "What are we supposed to do with failure, Lord," I asked. And my mind went over guys like Juggy who went back to dope five times before he really made it. I knew that Mom Rosado back in the Bronx was estimating that four out of five junkies who had a conversion experience were able to stay clean. And then there were the Curtises. But why didn't the Curtises become the Juggys? A lot of guys went back two, three, four times before they really let go of that last little shred of desire, and let God fill them with His Spirit.

"Don't let Curtis die, God. Don't let him go to the very end before he learns the way to live."

I pulled the sheet over my head to keep out the daylight, but I didn't sleep even though I was dead tired. My mind kept reaching out to all the miracles, all the "new men in Christ" who were learning how to live.

Jerry, right there beside me, was learning how to enter into the hidden needs of other people and to help them feel the power and compassion of Jesus Christ. He was a good leader. The guys like him. Joe, was out on the road, leading a group of all new fellows. Him and me were buddies at camp — used to sneak wine and read poetry. God's chipped him down; he's got the ability and the love too. Smart guy — but he's God's man now. God and him got things hooked up real tough. Mike—little kid with wounds across his stomach and scars on his face. Shot it out on a corner with a cop once, just on a dare.

Now he'll dare anything for Jesus. Chuck too — never knew what it was to be afraid. Fought with the tough gangs since he was a kid. Now he's almost forty years old, and it's beautiful to watch him working for God with all his heart. I see the anxiety in his face for the man he's bringing to Jesus. He just walks out on the street and starts talking to an addict, telling him about God.

The boys paraded like right across my bed — boys I knew in the Bronx and new boys too. Boys from Baltimore, Hartford, Vancouver, Portland, Cincinnati, Tampa, Denver, Chicago, Los Angeles, London. And girls. Little girls, fifteen or sixteen years old and too-wise women. Dona, Vicki, Connie, Beverly. It seemed there was no end. And over all the figures who passed through my mind I could see Curtis' face. Tears of disappointment and tears of thanksgiving flowed down my face into the pillow as I cried,

"Lord, save Curtis. Protect him. Get him up tight with You—like the other junkies You delivered."

Somewhere down the hall I heard singing,

"I asked the Lord to comfort me
When things weren't going my way,
He said to me, 'I will comfort you,
And lift your cares away."

The sound came closer and passed by our door. It was our song—the one we use at the end of our drama. One of the guys was singing on his way to work.

"I asked the Lord to walk with me,
When darkness was all that I knew,
He said to me, 'Never be afraid,
For I will see you through.' "

I rolled over and started to sing too, softly so I wouldn't wake Jerry.

"I didn't ask for riches,
He gave me wealth untold,
The moon, the stars, the sun, the sky,
And gave me eyes to behold.

I thank the Lord for ev'rything,
And I count my blessings each day,
He came to me when I needed Him,
I only had to pray,
And He'll come to you if you ask Him to,
He's only a pray'r away."

The sky like opened up and peace and assurance flowed into my mind and my heart and my body. Something warm come over me. I felt like God had just opened up the ceiling and come down to take me by the hand. I lay still in the wonderful relief. The tears stopped and deep inside the love of Jesus spread through me. The last thing I remember thinking before I went to sleep was, "Curtis, you'll make it, man! Don't you forget it! Jesus is higher than high!"